D1644939
UNIVE... HAM
WITHDRAWN
ROM THE LIBRAR

THE ECONOMICS OF BUILDING

THE ECONOMICS OF BUILDING

BY

HERBERT W. ROBINSON

Ph.D.(Econ.), F.S.S.

LONDON

P. S. KING & SON, LTD.

ORCHARD HOUSE, WESTMINSTER

1939

Published with the aid of a grant from the University of London Publication Fund

PRINTED AND BOUND IN GREAT BRITAIN BY RICHARD CLAY AND COMPANY, LTD.,
BUNGAY, SUFFOLK.

TO

MY FATHER AND MOTHER

PREFACE

THIS short monograph on the economics of building is a condensation of a thesis for the degree of Doctor of Philosophy in the University of London which was written in 1935–37, while the author held a Leverhulme Research Studentship at the London School of Economics. The original thesis was a much more detailed study, and readers wishing to do so may consult it in the library of the London School of Economics or in the Goldsmiths' Library of the University of London. The present monograph contains, however, important additional theoretical and statistical sections which have been worked out in the two years 1937–39 in Oxford.

Throughout the whole of my work at the London School of Economics I had the benefit of the stimulating criticism and helpful suggestions of my advisers. For the first year Professor Bowley was my adviser and provided most valuable suggestions in the early stages of the work. In the second Professor Arnold Plant and Mr. R. G. D. Allen jointly gave me the benefit of their supervision. Professor Plant made many helpful suggestions and was invaluable in keeping my analysis close to reality when I might have tended to stray too far into mere theoretical and mathematical speculation. Mr. Allen also proved extremely valuable in suggesting improvements in the general equilibrium analysis. Dr. E. C. Rhodes discussed the statistical problems with me in his seminar on methods of statistical investigation, and these discussions were of great value.

Dr. C. Oswald George has been specially helpful to me during the whole time and has generously discussed every problem considered. I wish to record my gratitude for his innumerable suggestions and criticisms and for the unfailing wisdom of his advice. Finally, discussions with many fellow students have been useful and stimulating.

HERBERT W. ROBINSON.

Oxford,
May 1939.

CONTENTS

INTRODUCTION

THE problems discussed within these pages are not the easiest in applied economics and statistics. Indeed, it would be hard to find many subjects which present more difficulties either in the selection of the mode of analysis or in the actual working out of the problems which arise.

The source of most of our difficulties can be traced to the fact that we are trying to make generalisations about essentially heterogeneous goods and activities. In fact this study might truly be called a study in heterogeneity. Buildings are essentially heterogeneous and, to be strictly accurate, every building should be regarded as being different from all others. It is true that some buildings are very much alike, physically, but even then there are great differences in geographical position and this attribute is of the greatest importance in the economics of building.

Furthermore, the classes concerned in this sphere of economic life, such as manual workers in the industry, contractors, speculative builders, investors, owner-occupiers, and rent-payers, differ widely in their functions, yet one person may take on several different rôles simultaneously (*e.g.* when the owner-occupier supplies his own house by building it himself). This introduces further elements of heterogeneity and complicates the problems correspondingly. Finally, the factors concerned are very numerous and inter-related in a bewildering manner. They bring about many complex problems such as the "need" for houses, the proportion of unoccupied houses, the relation between capital cost, repairs and alterations and the life of buildings, demolition and replacement of buildings, and so on. It is clear, therefore, that the problem of analysing the economic phenomena connected with the building industry is full of pitfalls and is, by the very nature of the persons and goods considered, not capable of rigorous analysis unless certain arbitrary classifications are adopted.

The final solution to our problems was only found after

many vain attempts to plan our analysis. The method finally selected was that of starting with a consideration of the conditions required for a stationary economy. Then the effects of each group of factors which influence building are investigated by allowing these factors to vary, one group at a time, while the rest remain constant. In the case of economic factors, the problem is divided into the determination of rents, the determination of prices of buildings and the determination of building costs; this was found to simplify the analysis.

Much of the economics of building may be extended to other industries, particularly when those industries are producing consumers' durable goods or even durable goods generally. For instance in a Note to Chapter II the determination of the length of life of buildings is analysed, and the effects of changes in interest rates on the length of life of buildings are investigated. This analysis is applicable to almost all durable goods and it is hoped that students will find it useful for the general theory of investment and capital. Again, in Chapter V, the problem of showing how the determinants of building activity operate involves the elaboration of a technique relating three markets: the market for buildings for occupation, the market for buildings for ownership, and the market for building activity. This theory is applicable to all economic goods and is particularly useful when stocks of commodities exist (*i.e.* when there is a market for ownership).

The statistical section of the book, Chapters VII and VIII, tests the theoretical results of the preceding chapters. Chapter VII deals with demographic factors and amply justifies the theory. It also makes an attempt to forecast the long run tendency of residential building in the future. Chapter VIII applies modern statistical method to economic factors in both residential building and factory and commercial building. Here again the theory proves sufficient to explain the extent of building in these two categories. It is found that a few factors alone are really important.

Although this book is written primarily for the student of economics and statistics certain sections (Chapters I–V, and the general principles of analysis) will, it is hoped, prove palatable to the lay reader. Throughout the statistical analysis the whole of the country is considered, but the same analysis may be applied to smaller areas. It is possible for anyone, using the Census of Population, the annual reports of the Registrar-General, and local data concerning rents, costs of building and rates of interest, to make the same analysis for local residential building developments. It follows, therefore, that persons engaged in the building industry (*e.g.* speculative builders, estate agents and architects), might profitably apply some of this analytical and statistical technique to their own local business problems.

CHAPTER I

THE BUILDING INDUSTRY AND ITS ECONOMIC SETTING

I. Preliminary Considerations

To define "the building industry" is by no means a simple task, and different writers have naturally used the term in different senses according to their needs and aims.

The industry is usually subdivided into "Building" and "Public Works Contracting." "Building" includes the erection and maintenance of houses, factories, and commercial buildings, including shops, offices, places of entertainment, railway stations, etc., while "Public Works Contracting" includes the construction and maintenance of roads, bridges, canals, tunnels, harbours, etc., for local or central governments.

"Construction" may be taken to include the erection of any structure or the alteration of the natural topography of the ground, plus the maintenance and repair of such products.

The building industry is peculiar in that it is the only industry producing goods which cannot be transferred from one place to another, a fact which implies that the industry cannot be concentrated in any small area, but must be as dispersed as the population whose needs it serves. For this reason it is also "sheltered" from foreign competition, but on the other hand it cannot expand its market by exporting its products. Another important fact is that raw materials used in construction (sand, gravel, chalk, clay, bricks, etc.) are very heavy, and therefore costly to transport. Since these materials are fairly evenly distributed over the country, high transport costs relatively to the value of the product imply that the raw materials industries too are as dispersed as geological conditions allow. Furthermore, the building industry is one which uses male labour only and requires a high proportion of labour to raw materials. Finally, building activity is dependent to a very large extent upon weather conditions, and the industry is therefore seasonal.[1]

2. The Growing Importance of the Building Industry

The building industry holds a key position in the modern economy. Because the population needs houses and almost every field of production requires buildings of some description, the building industry itself actually accounts for a large proportion of the national production of goods and services, and a vast army of men is required in the business of construction alone. But, in addition, whatever the structure, large quantities of different materials, bricks, cement, stone, gravel, chalk, timber, many metal products and numerous fittings, are required for its construction and are brought from widely distributed areas within the country and from abroad. Further, when the building is erected a large number of complementary products and fittings (furniture, electrical apparatus, machinery, and ancillary services such as gas and water) are required before it is ready for occupation, whether as a home or as a factory or commercial building. The building industry has, therefore, very wide ramifications both spatially and industrially, and the number of workers engaged in building and allied industries is very considerable. From the Occupations volumes of the Censuses of Population 1881–1931[2] it appears that the building industry (Building and Works of Construction) has accounted for 8–11% of the total occupied male population of England and Wales over the last fifty years. But it is subject to very violent fluctuations in size; in 1891 it accounted for 9·06%

[1] This aspect of the building industry (seasonal fluctuations) will be neglected in this study, but the reader is referred to C. T. Saunders, *Seasonal Variations in Employment*, and Horst Mendershausen, "The Elimination of Seasonal Fluctuations in the Building Industry", *International Labour Review*, August 1937, and *Les Variations du Mouvement Saisonnier dans l'Industrie de la Construction*", for further discussion of the subject.

[2] The volumes are strictly comparable from 1881 to 1911, but a complete revision of definitions of occupations occurred in 1921. Even then fairly comparable figures can be compiled for the building industry.

of the occupied male population, in 1901 this figure had risen to 11·09%, and in 1911 it had fallen to 8·26%. In the post-war decade 1921–31 it rose from 8·04% to 9·64%. The variations in the absolute numbers occupied in the industry show even more striking variations: 798,000 in 1891, 1,126,000 in 1901, 946,000 in 1911, all these referring to males over 10 years of age. In 1921 the number of males over 12 years of age occupied in building was 974,000, and in 1931 the number over 14 years of age was 1,277,000.

To examine the post-war development more closely, let us examine the Unemployment Insurance figures relating to the number of insured persons in employment in different industries [1] in 1924, 1929, and 1936. Though the absolute numbers in various industries may not be comparable over the whole period owing to legislative and administrative changes in insurance conditions, the proportions in various industries are more comparable, since there have been no really important changes in the scope of insurance.

TABLE I

Employment in the Building and Associated Industries. (Great Britain and Northern Ireland).

Source: Ministry of Labour Gazette.

Industry.	June 1924.[2]		June 1929.		June 1936.	
	Number Employed.	% of Total Persons Employed. in all Industries.	Number Employed.	% of Total Persons Employed in all Industries.	Number Employed.	% of Total Persons Employed in all Industries.
Building	658,120	6·31	755,740	6·91	910,730	7·83
Public Works	114,440	1·10	134,630	1·23	177,050	1·52
Building Materials [1]	165,650	1·58	190,410	1·74	243,560	2·09
Sawmilling (and Machined Woodwork)	52,470	0·50	53,430	0·49	55,910	0·48
Furniture-making (Upholstering, etc.)	90,800	0·94	113,370	1·04	130,370	1·12
Total	1,081,480	10·43	1,247,580	11·41	1,517,620	13·04
All Industries	10,423,480	100·0	10,931,340	100·0	11,631,160	100·0

[1] Composed of: Stone Quarrying and Mining; Slate Quarrying and Mining; Clay, Sand, Gravel and Chalk Pits; Artificial Stone and Concrete; Cement, Limekilns and Whiting; Brick, Tile, Pipe, etc., Making; Paint, Varnish, Red Lead, etc.
[2] Aged 16 and over.

[1] Taken from the *Ministry of Labour Gazette*.

From Table I it is clear that the building and contracting industry occupies a very important position in the economy, and has shown a remarkable increase in importance from 1924 to 1936. The percentage of the British insured population employed in Building and Public Works Contracting shows an increase from 7·4% in 1924 to 9·4% in 1936,[1] most of this increase occurring between 1929 and 1936, two fairly comparable years in the trade cycle.

The percentage of the British insured population engaged in the Building Materials industry, increased from 1·6% in 1924 to 2·1% in 1936. This increase was continuous over the period, although individual industries within the group changed in importance. Sawmilling shows a slight decline in the percentage of the British working population engaged therein, while Furniture-Making increased from 0·94% in 1924 to 1·12% in 1936.

The percentage engaged in all the industries combined increased from 10·43% in 1924 to 11·41% in 1929 and to 13·04% in 1936. This shows the great importance of the building industry and its immediately associated industries for the level of employment, and the remarkable extent to which the relative importance of these industries has been enhanced in post-war years,[2] particularly between 1929 and 1936. An indication of the importance of the building industry alone, excluding public works and all other associated industries, in the recovery 1932–7 is that, although it accounted for only 6·7% of the insured population of Great Britain and Northern Ireland in July 1932, it increased its insured workers by 21% in this period (the average for all industries was 7%) and accounted for 12·5% of the total

[1] The percentage of all insured workers attached to Building and Public Works Contracting increased from 7·44% in 1924 to 9·81% in 1936, an even greater increase.

[2] According to the *Year-book of the Building Industries National Council*, the industries (i) directly dependent upon, (ii) partly dependent upon, and (iii) indirectly affected by, the building industry together accounted for 1,499,000 persons in insured employment in July 1936. The building industry and the public works and contracting industry accounted for another 1,088,000, so that together these trades were responsible for 2,587,000 persons, or 22% of the insured persons in employment. These estimates include many trades not included in the table given above, since many of them produce only a small part of their output for the building industry or for the equipment of buildings.

increase in insured persons in employment. The "building boom" of 1932–7 must, however, not be regarded as without precedent. The increase in the number of workers engaged in building since 1932 has probably failed to bring the proportion of Britain's workers in the industry above the level of 1901. Neither has the expansion of the industry during this period exceeded that which occurred between 1891 and 1901.

3. Firms in the Building Industry

Firms in the building industry can be placed in four main classes.

The "*general contractor*" contracts for the largest type of building and sometimes for civil engineering work. He is called a public works contractor if he contracts for public authorities, and probably styles himself general and public works contractor. He contracts directly with the would-be-owner, who may be a public authority, for the entire work on a project, and is legally responsible for the execution of the whole work, usually doing some part of the actual construction with his own staff and equipment. He is mainly concerned, however, with the co-ordination of the work of the numerous sub-contractors who specialise in some particular phase of the erection and completion of the building. These general contractors execute local contracts mainly, but occasionally tender for contracts outside their locality.

The small "general contractor" who contracts for buildings of only moderate size is very similar to the large contractor above, and differs only in that he executes a much larger proportion of the work himself, probably subletting only such operations as require patent installations or methods. He does not, as a rule, undertake speculative building, but will often undertake maintenance and remodelling work.

Although these two groups are small in number compared with the total number of building firms, they execute a predominant part by value of the total building work, particularly in industrial, commercial and public building.

The "*jobbing builder*", the "small master builder" and the "master workman" undertake repair work, remodelling, painting and decorating almost exclusively, and rarely erect new buildings. These firms are highly localised and very small (in London they average 5–20 men employed at one time), although they form a very high percentage of the total number of firms. Their work is mainly confined to their immediate neighbourhood, since they have not the capital, equipment, or training to operate in more than a small area, and the size of the individual firm varies greatly according to the volume of business on hand.

The "*speculative builder*" ("owner builder" and "operative builder" are synonymous) is himself owner and builder; he concentrates on residential building, and either sells the finished structure to a purchaser or operates it himself at a profit. The general procedure followed by speculative builders is as follows. A "land jobber", sometimes the speculative builder himself, acquires land which he considers will be valuable for building, and lays it out for building purposes by constructing streets and sewers. The speculative builder, if he considers houses are really required, then buys or leases a number of building sites, often paying only a deposit and arranging to pay the balance after selling the houses he intends to build. He then draws up plans (either doing this himself or employing an architect), paying due regard to regulations regarding number of houses per acre, size of rooms, drainage and so on, has them passed by the local authority, and commences to build. Often the speculative builder has insufficient resources to finance the whole project himself and has to borrow capital; usually he obtains a bank overdraft, but sometimes he is able to arrange a loan elsewhere. He next obtains his materials from the brickmaker, timber merchant, and builder's merchant, who first protect themselves by arranging that the persons financing the builder guarantee payment of their accounts.

Having erected the houses, he either raises a mortgage on the property and pays off the loan, keeping the houses as an investment, or he sells the houses outright to investors or owner-occupiers. Often the completed houses are mortgaged through a building society for the buyers, though in most cases the buyers will arrange this independently. The builder's profit depends, obviously, on the difference between the selling price and the costs incurred.

The size of the firm varies greatly according to the extent of the building undertaken, and the regular staff of such firms is small; in London rarely more than 50 men are employed at any one time, and usually only 12 to 15. Very often a large amount of sub-contracting work is let out, all the brickwork, plastering, and painting being let by the piece to other firms. In this respect the speculative builders resemble the general contractors described above.

Finally there are the "*sub-contractors*" who contract to execute some section of the construction of the building for general contractors or speculative builders. There is, in this country, no general rule as to what work is let to sub-contractors, consequently there are many different types of firm, from the very large firm undertaking wrecking and excavating to the small electrician undertaking the installation of a lighting system for a speculative builder. Much building work is sub-let because it demands very specialised skill or knowledge. Examples of such work are wrecking, excavating, steel erection, concreting, stonework, carpentering, plastering, heating and plumbing, electrical work, and even painting. It is obvious, from this very brief description of building firms, that the building industry consists of a large number of small but highly specialised firms all competing with each other for building work.

Some indication of the size of the firms and the variations to be found are provided by the Censuses of Production of 1924 and 1930.[1] It is officially estimated in the 1924 Census that most of the 13,000 firms supplying no particulars

[1] For a more detailed analysis of the output of the building trades, the structure of the industry and the importance of the small firms see "Investment in the Building Industry, 1930–1935," by I. Bowen, *Review of Economic Studies*, Vol. 6, Nos. 2 and 3.

were small firms, and that 40,000 persons were employed in these firms but not recorded. In the 1930 Census almost all of the 3,950 firms supplying no particulars were small and, assuming three persons per firm (as in 1924), we can roughly estimate that 12,000 persons were employed in small firms. Adjusting the published figures in this way we obtain the results shown in Table II.[1]

TABLE II

Size of Firm in the Building Industry.

Source: Censuses of Production 1924 and 1930.

	1924.			1930.		
	More than 10 Employees.	Less than 10 Employees.	Total.	More than 10 Employees.	Less than 10 Employees.	Total.
Number of Firms	9,500	40,400	49,900	8,330	43,620	51,950
Persons employed	410,638	135,343	545,981	444,538	166,341	610,879
Percentage of Total	75·2	24·8	100	72·8	27·2	100
Average Number of persons employed	43·23	3·35	10·94	53·37	3·81[1]	11·76

[1] The preliminary reports of the 1935 Census of Production indicate a further remarkable increase in the number of small firms (by 36%) to 59,100. The average number of persons employed was, however, 3·64 as against a comparable average of 3·88 in 1930.

The total number of persons employed increased by about 12% from 1924 to 1930, the number of persons employed in firms with less than ten employees increasing by 23% and in the larger businesses by 8%. From the table it is seen that the small firms increased their share of the total persons employed in the industry; it rose from 24·8% to 27·2%. This shows the still growing importance of the small firm in the building industry, and that the advance in employment occurred to a greater extent in businesses of this type. Assuming that all the 13,000 firms omitted in 1924 were small firms, the number of firms employing more than 10 persons was 9,500, and the number employing fewer

[1] The discrepancy between the "total number of persons employed" in this table and the figure given in Table I is due to the fact that the scope of the Census of Production is different from the scope of the Ministry of Labour figures. Moreover, the numbers recorded as employed in Public Utility Services for the purposes of unemployment insurance include workpeople engaged in certain services that are excluded from the Census.

than 10 persons was 40,400. In 1930, making the assumption that the 3,950 firms omitted were small, the figures are 8,330 and 43,620. Thus, while the large firms decreased in number by 12%, the small firms increased in number by 8%.

What of the average size of the firms? Table II shows (i) that the average size of a firm is only 11·8 persons per firm; (ii) that the average size of the unit increased in both types of firm, the average size of the unit in the whole industry increasing from 10·9 to 11·8; (iii) that, while the average size of the small firm showed an increase of about 14% (3·4–3·8) the average size of the larger firms increased by about 23% (43·2–53·4), and the latter account for practically the whole of the increase in size. It should be noted that these figures refer to Great Britain and Northern Ireland, that they include persons of all ages, and that they are average figures over the whole year.

Finally we turn to the distribution of firms by size. Unfortunately, there are no figures before 1930, and those for 1930 only cover in detail those firms employing more than 10 persons, *i.e.*, only about 16% of the total number of firms. The distribution obtained, however, is as follows, and shows the great predominance of the small firm. Only 4·2% of firms employ more than 50 persons and only 1·6% employ more than 100.

Size of Firm. Average Nos. Employed.	Estimated Number of Firms.	%.
0–10	43,620	83·8
11–24	3,749	7·2
25–49	2,480	4·8
50–99	1,339	2·6
100–199	549	1·0
200–499	263	0·5
500 and over	54	0·1
Total . . .	51,954	100·0

In view of the very large number of small firms in the building industry it is justifiable to say that conditions approaching those of the economist's " perfect competition " rule in this industry. On the other hand, the raw materials industries are distinguished by monopolies and cartels, for "imperfect competition" rules in the brick, cement, and timber industries as well as in some of the industries producing metal products used in building.

4. Trades Engaged in the Building Industry

The labour engaged in the building industry is drawn from a variety of occupations, many of them highly skilled. The workers involved are bricklayers, carpenters and

TABLE III

Building : Occupations.

Occupation.	June 1924.[1]		June 1929.[1]		June 1936.[1]		1911[2] Census.	1931[2] Census.
	Numbers Employed.	% of all Employed.	Numbers Employed.	% of all Employed.	Numbers Employed.	% of all Employed.	% of All Occupied.	% of All Occupied.
Skilled . .	254,370	38·5	276,050	36·5	331,760	36·4	48·6	39·8
Carpenters and Joiners	122,570	18·6	120,770	16·0	136,810	15·0	22·2	19·3
Bricklayers.	56,650	8·6	73,970	9·8	94,940	10·4	10·9	9·3
Masons .	21,870	3·3	21,400	2·8	20,820	2·3	5·0	3·0
Slaters .	4,980	0·7	5,800	0·8	8,010	0·9	0·9	0·6
Plasterers .	15,860	2·4	23,030	3·0	33,050	3·6	2·7	2·6
Plumbers .	32,440	4·9	31,080	4·1	38,130	4·2	6·9	5·0
Semi-Skilled :								
Painters .	100,000	15·2	102,010	13·5	125,400	13·8	19·9	16·2
Unskilled : .								
Labourers and Miscellaneous.	303,760	46·3	377,680	50·0	453,570	49·8	31·5	44·0
Total .	658,130	100·0	755,740	100·0	910,730	100·0	100·0	100·0

[1] Numbers of insured workers 16–64 recorded in employment in the *Ministry of Labour Gazette* (in 1924, 16 years and over).
[2] Numbers recorded in Occupations volume of Census of Population (1911 over 10 years of age, 1931 over 14 years of age).

joiners, painters, plasterers, masons, slaters and tilers, plumbers, and many specialised workers such as electricians and gas-fitters. Finally, to all these skilled workers there are labourers; these are not completely unskilled and, indeed, often possess quite an extensive knowledge of skilled operations. For instance, contrary to general opinion the navvy is quite a skilled worker.

Table III sets out the distribution of workers in building and works of construction among different occupations.

The figures for 1924, 1929, and 1936 are taken from Unemployment Insurance statistics and refer to *employed* persons, while those for 1911 and 1931 are taken from the Occupations volumes of the Census of Population and refer to all persons "*occupied*". There is, therefore, no strict basis of comparison between the two sets of data. The main groups are skilled workers, unskilled workers, and painters (semi-skilled), the skilled section being further subdivided into the various trades.

Among the skilled workers the predominance of carpenters, joiners and bricklayers is very marked. They account for about 25% of all insured workers since 1924. Bricklayers have increased in importance (from 8·6% to 10·4%) from 1924 to 1936, carpenters and joiners dropped steadily from 18·6% to 15·0%, and so did masons (3·3% to 2·3%). Plasterers substantially increased in importance (2·4% to 3·6%), plumbers fell off slightly, and so did painters. On the other hand, "labourers and miscellaneous" increased from 46·3% to 49·8%. Taking the three main divisions, there is a clear falling off in the percentage of skilled workers employed (38·5% to 36·4%), a falling off in the percentage of semi-skilled workers (15·2% to 13·8%), and an increase in the percentage of unskilled workers (46·3% to 49·8%), and unless the change in the census proportions is completely unreliable, these tendencies are even more marked over the period 1911–31. The astonishing growth in the importance of the unskilled worker (31·5% to 44·0%) is probably connected with the introduction of new materials and new methods of production over this period, although it must be remembered that the general labourer has often become a kind of semi-skilled mechanic, handling new apparatus such as pneumatic drills and mechanical mixers. It is significant, perhaps, that this increase in unskilled work has been attended by the decline of the old apprentice system, and that methods of recruitment of labour have remained very haphazard.[1]

[1] For a full analysis of recruitment of labour in London see R. G. D. Allen and B. Thomas, "The London Building Industry and its Labour Recruitment through Employment Exchanges," *Economic Journal*, September 1937.

Wages are fixed according to a scale of wages agreed upon throughout the industry, and the whole scale is adjusted according to the cost of living. There are, however, deviations from these standard rates, and in practice there still exists a certain degree of flexibility in wages from time to time and from area to area.

5. Changes in the Building Industry

There have been very great changes in the organisation of the building industry during the last twenty years. During the major part of the nineteenth century, and particularly in the case of residential building, the greater part of the actual building operations from the laying out of the foundations to the papering and decorating was carried out by one builder or general contractor. But with the introduction of steel and concrete into building technique and the increasing complexity of construction, there has arisen a new type of general contractor possessing business, organising, and engineering ability, and a new type of firm, resembling a factory in its organisation and mainly concerned with the co-ordination of the work of a number of specialised sub-contractors. These subsidiary firms have increased in number and degree of specialisation as the masonry, structural steel, woodwork, new materials, and fittings have demanded more and more specialised knowledge. The number of these sub-contractors engaged on one building is, in some cases, as high as thirty. Since each sub-contractor is a separate entrepreneur, there is an increased distribution of risk and responsibility for the storage of materials, capital investment, and labour management. The large general contractor of today merely takes on the function of general organiser for the entire project.

The building industry is changing from one based on tradition to one based on the application of scientific research; new materials and systems of construction are constantly being introduced. Technical methods of construction are altering rapidly, owing largely to the desire for speed: since the War the time required for building in large construction projects has been reduced by 30% or 40%. Steel-frame erection is being adopted to an increasing extent, and enables the ground floor to be completed before the rest of the building, therefore reducing the time required before the building can be used. Ferro-concrete is being used extensively, since it is a much more flexible material to work with than stone or brickwork, and cement has been substituted for mortar. Seasonal stoppages have been reduced both by the use of braziers and artificial light, and by the erection of the roof at an early stage in building. Machinery has been extensively applied, particularly in the early stages; such appliances as brickmaking machinery, hydraulic and pneumatic riveters, rock drills, steam shovels, hoisting engines, power mixers, woodworking machinery, and the cement gun and paint spray are now used. Another development is the manufacture of wood and metal building parts in factories and workshops and their fixing into the building by semi-skilled workers; for instance, metal doors and windows, wooden doors and cupboards, and so on, are now produced and fitted in this way.

However, in the old basic trades of bricklaying, joinering, etc., the general serving of materials and the use of mechanical aids to reduce fatigue show little change; for instance, the speed of a bricklayer has not changed greatly during the last fifty years. The work of masons, slaters, tilers, plasterers, carpenters, and painters is still mainly a hand operation, even on the largest buildings, and mechanical methods are rarely applied.

The effects of these changes on the building trades have been marked. Carpenters have suffered from the use of manufactured woodwork, plumbers have suffered from the use of composition roofing in place of lead, and stonemasons and bricklayers from the use of steel-frame construction, ferro-concreting, artificial stone, girders faced with brick and stone, and so on. All trades have been characterised by increasing specialisation as a result of the introduction of new processes and new materials, and specialists are taking the place of the ordinary artisan and navvy. Finally, entirely new methods have developed new trades such as concrete shutterers, steel benders and fixers, concrete mixers, etc. These changes are, however, less marked in the case of residential building, where the new methods have found little application except in the case of large blocks of flats or tenement houses.

6. The Main Economic Features of the Building Industry

From the economist's point of view, the following are the main features revealed by this brief description of the building industry.

(1) The building industry is a local industry, except in a few exceptional cases, and is distributed largely according to the distribution of population and industry; there is no concentration into special areas, as, for instance, in the case of the Lancashire cotton industry. The raw materials industries are more concentrated than the building industry because they depend on the natural distribution of materials, but there can be no concentration in one region.

(2) The building industry is a good example of a " sheltered " industry; there is no question of foreign competition except in the case of the raw materials industries, where there is some import of semi-manufactured products, timber, stone, slates, bricks, and so on. On the other hand, it cannot expand by entering other markets abroad.

(3) The size of the firms in the building industry, the raw materials industries, and the complementary industries varies from the very biggest type of firm down to the smallest. In the building industry itself there is a close approach to perfect competition, as in the speculative building of houses for instance, while in the raw materials industries, particularly in the cement industry, there is an approach to perfect monopoly.

(4) There are two essentially different types of firm in the industry. One type, the general contractor, the sub-contractor, and the jobbing builder, sells the building before construction by working to contract, and therefore bears little risk. The other type, the speculative builder, produces

the building before selling it, and thus bears speculative risks.

(5) The industry produces a special type of product—namely, a highly durable good whose durability depends upon its construction. It is doubly interesting since it produces both durable producers' goods and durable consumers' goods.

(6) These products (*i.e.* buildings) are produced to accommodate industries in all stages of the production of consumption goods, from the extraction of raw materials, through the whole process of production, to the final distribution to the consumer.

(7) The building industry is one in which both skilled and unskilled labour is employed and labour costs form an important part of the total costs of building, though, as we have seen, machinery and mechanical appliances are becoming more and more common. Building is almost exclusively a male occupation.

(8) The building industry is one of special interest, since employment in so many trades and industries depends directly or indirectly upon building activity. Employment, not only in the building trades themselves, but also in the raw materials industries and those industries producing complementary products (furniture, textiles, etc.) is dependent on the volume of building.

(9) Employment in the building industry is subject to seasonal fluctuations because building activity depends on weather conditions and social factors. Also, owing to the organisation of the industry, the activity of an individual firm is very irregular, as its work usually depends upon success in obtaining contracts or selling houses.

We now leave the organisation of the industry and approach the problem of disentangling the various factors which dictate the demands made at any one moment upon the services of the industry. In the next chapter we build up the conditions for a stationary state with respect to building activity. In the subsequent chapters the effects upon building activity of changes in the various relevant demographic and economic variables are investigated and finally measured.

CHAPTER II

A STATIONARY STATE WITH RESPECT TO BUILDING ACTIVITY

1. Introduction

In a modern capitalistic economy the factors relevant to the determination of building activity are both numerous and complex. They are inter-related in a bewildering manner, and it is difficult, therefore, to analyse them in a logical and systematic way. However, to bring out clearly what factors are involved, and how they operate, let us examine what extreme assumptions would have to be made for a stationary economy in which no addition to the number and types of buildings in existence would be required, and in which the amount of building activity per unit of time would be stationary. It may be argued that such procedure is so unreal that results based upon it can have no importance for real life, that it is merely an exercise in theoretical economics possessing no more than entertainment value. But if the problem were not simplified in this way, and we plunged immediately into an analysis of a dynamic economy, it would be almost impossible to disentangle the demographic and economic factors involved. We therefore set up this stationary economy, without claiming that it represents the real world, in order that we may be able subsequently to introduce dynamic changes one by one and so arrive finally at a comprehensive dynamic analysis.

In the theoretical analysis the term "house" means a family accommodation, where "family" is defined as a person or group of persons who would, in the absence of any economic or social restraints, occupy a "structurally separate dwelling". We can use here the Census of Population definition of a structurally separate dwelling :—

"A structurally separate dwelling has been defined . . . as any room or set of rooms, intended or used for habitation, having separate access either to the street or to a common landing or staircase. Thus each flat in a block of flats is a separate unit;

a private house which has not been structurally subdivided is similarly a single unit, whether occupied by one family or several families. But where a private house has been subdivided into maisonettes or portions, each having its front door opening on to the street or on to a common landing or staircase to which visitors have access, then each such portion is treated as a separate unit."

The subjective definition of a family will be used throughout the theoretical analysis, but is replaced by objective definitions when we turn to statistical analysis.

Some of the assumptions which have to be made for the stationary economy may, at first sight, give an appearance of unreality, but the mere search for those necessary may be fruitful, in that light is thus thrown on the whole problem.

2. The Extreme Assumptions

(1) The first set of assumptions is

(*a*) That each house is physically identical with every other and that no changes occur in type or quality;

(*b*) That there is a constant number of families all of the same size, and a constant ratio of families to dwellings. The number of houses required depends upon the number of families in existence and the ratio of families per dwelling; and, morever, a family of a given size requires a house of a *particular* minimum size.[1] This means that the total population remains constant, which requires that at each point of time the total number of births is equal to the total number of deaths;

(*c*) That the tastes of the population, and particularly those in respect of houses, remain unchanged—this includes all habits and customs of society and is necessary because changes in tastes will lead to a demand for *new* houses of new types and to variations in building activity. It is, of course, difficult to say whether, in actual fact, changes in tastes lead to changes in house-design or vice versa.

[1] The two assumptions, that the number and size of families are constant, can be imagined, though it is highly improbable that they will ever be realised. Such unreality may be excused on the grounds that our assumptions are, after all, only temporary.

(2) The second set of assumptions is

(*a*) The incomes of all families are constant;
(*b*) The cost of living (apart from rent and rates) is constant;
(*c*) House-rent (apart from rates) is constant;
(*d*) Rates are constant.

These assumptions are required since, with given tastes, family expenditure on rent depends on the level of rent and rates, the cost of living, and family income; and in stationary equilibrium this expenditure is constant.

(3) The third assumption, which follows from the fact that houses cannot be moved, once built, but does not necessarily follow from assumption one, is that there are no spatial movements of population

(*a*) Into or out of the country;
(*b*) Internally from one district to another;
(*c*) From town to country or vice versa.

For if such movement occurs, new buildings are required in regions receiving population, and buildings are superfluous in regions losing population.

(4) There is no shifting of industries or dying out of industries. This is clearly connected with assumption three, of a stationary geographically fixed population.

(5) The fifth set of assumptions is

(*a*) That the initial quantity of building activity required to build, and the physical amount of repair work required per annum to maintain a house, are constant;

(*b*) That the costs of building activity are constant, therefore the cost of construction per house and costs of repairs per house are fixed;

(*c*) That the length of life of buildings is constant. This follows from the fact that the length of life of the houses is dependent upon the initial cost and expenditure annually on repairs and, since both are fixed, the length of life is also constant.

(6) The rate of interest is constant. Otherwise, as will be seen later, initial cost and expenditure annually on repairs might fluctuate.

(7) There are no fires, catastrophes, or " Acts of God ".

The only building activity which goes on in this stationary economy is as follows. First, since the amount of repair work per house per annum is constant, and there is a constant number of houses, the total amount of repair work carried out annually is constant. Secondly, as a house reaches the end of its useful life, by which we mean that further repair work is no longer considered profitable, it must be pulled down and rebuilt. Thus, in order to have a constant amount of building activity devoted to replacement, we must also have a final assumption;

(8) That the ages of houses are so distributed that an equal number are due for replacement each year, *i.e.* houses are equally distributed over each year of life.

Since a family must leave a home ready for demolition and enter one which has been rebuilt, there must obviously be (*a*) some slight movement of population to allow for this, unless houses are permanent, and (*b*) a larger number of sites for houses than there are families.

3. Residential Building activity in the Stationary State

Let L years be the length of life of a house from the moment when it is ready for habitation to the moment when it can no longer be inhabited. Let one year be required to demolish and rebuild the house.[1] Finally, let there be m families and one family per house, hence there are m houses.

Each year $\frac{m}{L}$ houses will need to be replaced, and this expression represents what may well be called the " replace-

[1] On the assumption that new houses are built on the old sites and take exactly one year to build, so that each year sufficient houses are built to accommodate those families moving from houses becoming obsolescent he number of sites required for m families is $\frac{m(L+1)}{L}$.

ment quota ". During each year, let $\frac{m}{L}$ houses be built to replace the $\frac{m}{L}$ which will require replacement in the next year, thus leaving m for habitation at every point of time. Thus, when a house is worn out it is demolished and rebuilt in one year in time to replace a house whose replacement is imminent.

Total building activity will, therefore, be stationary and equal to the sum of building activity devoted to replacement and building activity devoted to repairs.

4. Equilibrium between Initial Cost, Repair Work, and Length of Life

In the stationary economy considered above, it is reasonable to assume that the combination of initial cost of the building and annual repair work will be so chosen that the total annual cost required to house the population, measured as a quantity of building activity, will be a minimum.

Let " building activity " be considered as a homogeneous quantity measured in homogeneous units with constant value. Let us assume that, if the initial cost of removing an obsolescent house and constructing a new one is u units of building activity and the repair work is a constant amount v units of building activity per house per annum, the length of life $L = \phi\ (u,v)$ years, *i.e.* the length of life is a function of initial cost u and the amount of repair work v executed annually. It is important to notice that in actual life repairs are composed of two essentially different components. There are decorations required at very short intervals, say intervals of five years or less, and there are structural repairs, including exterior painting and pointing, which are required at longer intervals of, say, five, ten, twenty, or even thirty years. The former type are distinguished by the fact that they are not essential for comfortable habitation of the house and can therefore be delayed indefinitely without impairing the length of life of the building. On the other hand, the structural repairs cannot long be neglected without seriously shortening the length of life of the house. And if such repairs are neglected, the building will require even more extensive repairs in a short time. In all our theoretical analysis we shall confine our attention to the second type of repairs and include the first type in the same category as furniture. Even in the case of repairs which do lengthen the life of buildings, L cannot be increased indefinitely by expending more building activity on repairs, but that can be allowed for in the form of the function ϕ. We are also assuming here that repairs are constant in each year of the life of the house. In actual fact the repairs in the early years are much lower than those in subsequent years. However, we can imagine v to be that constant annual cost which gives a present discounted value, over the whole L years, equal to the present discounted value of repairs over the whole life of L years, however those actual repairs may fluctuate over time.

We have assumed that the number of houses required for the m families is m, and that therefore each year $\frac{m}{L}$ houses will be removed, and new buildings erected on the vacant sites.

The total building activity each year will then be:

Repair work on the m occupied houses ($= mv$ units), and

Replacement of the $\frac{m}{L}$ obsolete houses $\left(= \frac{mu}{L} \text{ units}\right)$.

The total annual building activity x will then be:

$$x = \frac{mu}{L} + mv \quad . \quad . \quad . \quad . \quad . \quad . \quad . \quad . \quad (1)$$

Assuming that initially m houses were built, costing mu units of building activity, the annual interest charge on these houses will be mui, where i is the constant rate of interest. There must also be an annual charge a for the amortisation of each house over the length of time $L + 1$ years.

The total annual cost y of m houses is therefore

$$y = mv + mui + ma \quad . \quad . \quad . \quad . \quad (2)$$

and u and v will be chosen in such a way that y is a minimum.

It is shown in the Note to this chapter that y is a minimum when the rate of substitution of annual capital cost for annual repair cost (the amount of annual capital cost which must be substituted for a lost unit of annual repair cost in order to leave the length of life of the building unchanged) is equal to unity, *i.e.*, when the addition of an equal expenditure to annual capital cost and to annual repairs results in equal additions to the length of life of the building. In addition, it is shown that in equilibrium both u and v, and therefore the length of life of the building L, depend upon (i) the rate of substitution of initial cost for repairs at different lengths of life L, and (ii) the rate of interest i. And finally it is shown that a fall in building costs or the rate of interest leads to an increase in the length of life. At the same time the initial cost u, the annual repair expenditure v, or both, will usually change, the only restriction being that both cannot *decrease* simultaneously.

The annual building activity, from (1), depends upon (i) the number of families and (ii) the length of life, initial cost of buildings, and the annual cost of repairs, all three of which depend upon the rate of substitution of annual initial cost for repairs, and the rate of interest.

5. Rents in the Stationary State

There will also be a unique relationship between rents, the length of life of the buildings, the rate of interest, and capital and maintenance costs.

Since all the factors (tastes, family income, cost of living) relevant to the determination of family expenditure on rent are constant, we can obviously assume that expectations regarding the future are, simply, that the present values of these variables will persist indefinitely.[1] Furthermore, these expectations will be held with perfect confidence. As the rate of interest is constant, we can also assume that the discounting of future receipts by entrepreneurs is at a discount rate equal to the rate of interest.

[1] In particular, since we assume a constant rate of interest, there will be no changes in expectations arising through this medium.

Consider an investor owning one single house which has a length of life of L years, an initial or replacement cost of u and an annual repair cost of v. Assume finally that he builds the house originally by raising a loan at the rate of interest i.

His annual charges are then,

(i) Interest upon initial capital expenditure $= ui$ annually.

(ii) Repairs $= v$ annually.

(iii) Amortisation for replacement over $L + 1$ years $= a = ui/[(1 + i)^{L+1} - 1]$ annually; and

(iv) His earnings which, in equilibrium, are just sufficient to induce him to engage in house-building $= c$, a constant, annually.

His annual gross receipts are the annual house-rent (apart from rates) $= z$.

He is discounting future rents at the rate of discount i when computing the present value of his receipts, and his annual costs will also be discounted at the same rate when he is computing the present value of the cost of the house. Since the present value of costs (including the minimum earnings) over L years must equal the present value of receipts, this means that he will equate his annual charges to his annual receipts. Thus:

$$z = ui + v + a + c$$

and since u, v, i, L, a, and c are constant, z is constant and determined by the rate of substitution of annual initial cost for repairs, and the rate of interest.

If the entrepreneur charges rates to the tenant in addition to the rent of the building, and pays them in turn to the local rating authority, the annual charge to the tenant will be supplemented by another constant quantity, say s, equal to the annual rates. If, on the other hand, the tenant pays the rates to the local authority himself, our equation will be comprehensive, but the tenant himself will pay z in house-rent plus s in rates.

6. Factory and Commercial Building in the Stationary State

We now consider what assumptions must be added to those already made to ensure a stationary amount of building activity with respect to factory and commercial buildings, which include factories, offices, shops, warehouses, etc. Those already made which are relevant to the problem are

(i) There is a constant number of families.
(ii) There is a constant family income. Hence the national income is constant.
(iii) Tastes are constant.
(iv) The cost of living is constant.
(v) Rents of houses are constant.
(vi) Rates are constant.
(vii) There is no spatial movement of population, a possible influence on factory location.
(viii) There is no shifting of industries.
(ix) Costs of building activity are constant.
(x) The rate of interest is constant.
(xi) There are no catastrophes, fires, or Acts of God.

But even these assumptions are not sufficient to guarantee a constant amount of building activity devoted to factory and commercial building. In addition to the assumption that there is no shifting of industries, we must also assume that no new industries appear and no industries disappear in any part of the economy, and that there is a rigid scheme of distribution of resources among different industries so that the proportion of buildings in each industry is not changing. This, and the assumptions above, imply that all prices, both of factors of production and consumption goods, remain constant.

Under these conditions the *capacity*[1] of the various industries in every part of the economy will be constant. However, owing to the fact that inventions may alter the type and size of buildings required to house any given

[1] Capacity in the sense of maximum possible output in physical terms.

capacity, we must also assume that there are no inventions or changes in methods of production. Thus, assuming an even distribution of factories, etc., by age, there will be a constant number of factories in existence at every moment of time and a constant amount of annual replacement activity with a constant amount of annual repair work.

The factors which determine the amount of annual replacement activity, the amount of annual repair work, and the total building activity are exactly analogous to the case of houses. Whereas in the case of dwellings the building houses a given family, in the case of factories, offices, etc., the building houses a given productive capacity. The annual building activity required to accommodate a given productive capacity will be made a minimum in the same way as for residential building. The length of life of factories, etc., and the constant amount of building activity devoted to factory and commercial building in our stationary economy depend once again upon the interaction of (i) the technical function relating length of life of buildings to initial cost and annual repair cost and (ii) the rate of interest.

The new sets of assumptions are then

(9) (*a*) No new industries appear and no industries disappear;

(*b*) There is constant productive capacity in all industries;

(*c*) All prices of factors of production and consumption goods are constant;

(*d*) There are no inventions or changes in methods of production.

(10) There is an even distribution of factories, offices, etc., by age.

In the case of public works exactly similar considerations apply, *i.e.*, there is a constant amount of annual replacement activity and a constant amount of annual repair expenditure.

7. Total Building Activity

In this stationary economy there is a constant amount of building activity for (*a*) houses, (*b*) factories and commercial buildings, and (*c*) public works. Since the total building activity is equal to the sum of the activity under each of these three heads, and the activity under each head is constant, there is a constant amount of building activity as a whole.[1]

These assumptions indicate how very numerous are the factors which influence building activity. In a dynamic economy all these factors may vary simultaneously; each factor plays a part in the determination of the tempo of building activity at any moment. The factors group themselves into two types, demographic factors and economic factors. In Chapter III the effects of demographic changes are considered, while Chapters IV and V are devoted to the effects of changing economic factors on building activity.

NOTE TO CHAPTER II

The Length of Life of Buildings and the Rate of Interest

The selection of the optimum length of life of buildings is a problem which finds its solution in the real world through trial and error. Imperishable structures are too expensive to construct, and very impermanent structures require too frequent replacement and too extensive running repairs. In practice a compromise is found which, considering initial cost, frequency of replacement and cost of repairs, is cheapest in the long run. It is obvious that the rate of interest plays an important part in this compromise, and it is interesting to analyse theoretically how its influence operates and what are the consequences of changes in the interest rate on the length of life of buildings. It is a problem concerning not only buildings but also any durable consumer's or producer's good. The length of life bears a close relationship to the "period of production" (average length of time between input and output) and the problem has, therefore, great importance for capital theory. Apart from Hicks' *Value and Capital*[2] there has been no attempt at a rigorous solution of

[1] Of course one might imagine an economy in which the total building activity x composed of three sections x_h, x_f, and x_p (houses, factories, public works) is constant, but where x_h, x_f, and x_p are varying. However, this would be a special case of a non-stationary economy, and it is sufficient merely to mention the possibility in this chapter.

[2] Chapter XVII, "Interest and the Production Plan", and Appendix to Chapter XVII.

the problem, and the solution offered here is, perhaps, of interest, since it makes use of a novel elaboration of the indifference curve technique.

Using the notation of pp. 22 to 26, the total annual cost y of m houses each with a length of life of L years is,

$$y = mui + mv + ma \quad . \quad . \quad . \quad . \quad . \quad (2)$$

where u is the initial cost of the building, measured in units of building activity, v is the annual repair expenditure per house, also in units of building activity, i is the rate of interest, and a is the annual amortisation quota, again in units of building activity. We are regarding a unit of building activity, therefore, as " money ".

The value of a is such that,

$$a(1 + i)^L + a(1 + i)^{L-1} + \ \ldots + a = u$$

hence
$$a = \frac{ui}{(\alpha - 1)}, \text{ where } \alpha = (1 + i)^{L+1} \quad . \quad . \quad (3)$$

Thus the total annual rent of the m houses is,

$$y = \frac{mui\alpha}{(\alpha - 1)} + mv \quad . \quad . \quad . \quad (4)$$

and must be a minimum. The conditions for a minimum are that $\frac{\partial y}{\partial u}$ and $\frac{\partial y}{\partial v}$ must be zero, *i.e.*

$$\frac{\partial L}{\partial u} = \frac{(\alpha - 1)}{u\beta} \quad . \quad . \quad . \quad . \quad . \quad . \quad (5)$$

and
$$\frac{\partial L}{\partial v} = \frac{(\alpha - 1)^2}{ui\alpha\beta} \quad . \quad . \quad . \quad . \quad . \quad . \quad (6)$$

where $\beta = \log_e (1 + i)$.

These two equations fully determine the two unknowns u and v, initial cost and annual repair cost. They therefore determine the length of life of the houses L, which is $\phi\ (u, v)$. Now

$$\frac{\frac{\partial L}{\partial v}}{\frac{\partial L}{\partial u}} = -\frac{du}{dv} = k \quad . \quad . \quad . \quad . \quad . \quad (7)$$

which is an important constant and represents the *rate of substitution of initial cost for annual repairs,* that is, the amount by which initial cost must increase to offset a decrease of one unit in annual repairs in order that the length of life L shall remain unchanged. This variable depends upon the length of life L and the values of u and v.

From equations (5) and (6),

$$k = \frac{(\alpha - 1)}{i\alpha} \quad . \quad . \quad . \quad . \quad . \quad (8)$$

Let u' be the annual cost of u units of initial cost, so that $u' = \frac{ui\alpha}{(\alpha - 1)}$. Thus $\frac{du'}{du} = \frac{i\alpha}{(\alpha - 1)}$ and

$$k \cdot \frac{du'}{du} = \frac{\frac{\partial L}{\partial v}}{\frac{\partial L}{\partial u'}} = -\frac{du'}{dv} = 1 \quad . \quad . \quad . \quad (9)$$

Hence in equilibrium $-\frac{du'}{dv}$ is unity. That is, the rate of substitution of *annual* capital cost for annual repairs is unity or, in other words, the addition of an equal amount to annual capital cost or to annual repairs results in equal additions to the length of life of the building. Equation (8) indicates that the length of life depends upon (i) the form of the function ϕ as expressed by the rate of substitution, and (ii) the rate of interest, i.[1]

The whole of this analysis may be simplified by making use of the indifference curve technique. And the effects of changes in building costs and the rate of interest on the length of life of buildings can be more easily shown diagrammatically.

Figure A in Figure 1 shows a series of length-of-life indifference curves all relating to a given size of house. Along the x axis is measured the amount of building activity expended on annual repairs, and along the y axis is measured the amount of building activity expended upon initial cost of the house. The

[1] The above analysis, and the length-of-life indifference curve analysis which follows, throw a great deal of light on the problems discussed in the recent controversy between Professor F. H. Knight and Mr. Nicholas Kaldor regarding the theory of capital (*Econometrica*, Vol. 5, No. 3; Vol. 6, No. 1; and Vol. 6, No. 2). In the general theory of capital our " initial cost " is the initial cost of capital equipment and our " annual repair expenditure " is the annual cost of production of a given output. The length of life of the building is, of course, the length of life of the capital equipment. The " investment period " of the capital required to produce the given output is, in our terminology,

$$\frac{L}{2}\left(1 + \frac{\sigma + 1}{\sigma + L}\right)$$

where σ (defined on p. 38) is the same as Mr. Kaldor's " capital intensity ".

It is doubtful, in view of the conclusions derived from the length-of-life indifference curve analysis which follows, whether Mr. Kaldor's analysis of " Capital Intensity and the Trade Cycle " in *Economica*, February, 1939, would be verified if the length-of-life indifference curve technique were used to investigate changes in σ during the trade cycle. It is hoped that the methods developed here will be extended to the theory of investment and capital, and to trade cycle theory, in the near future.

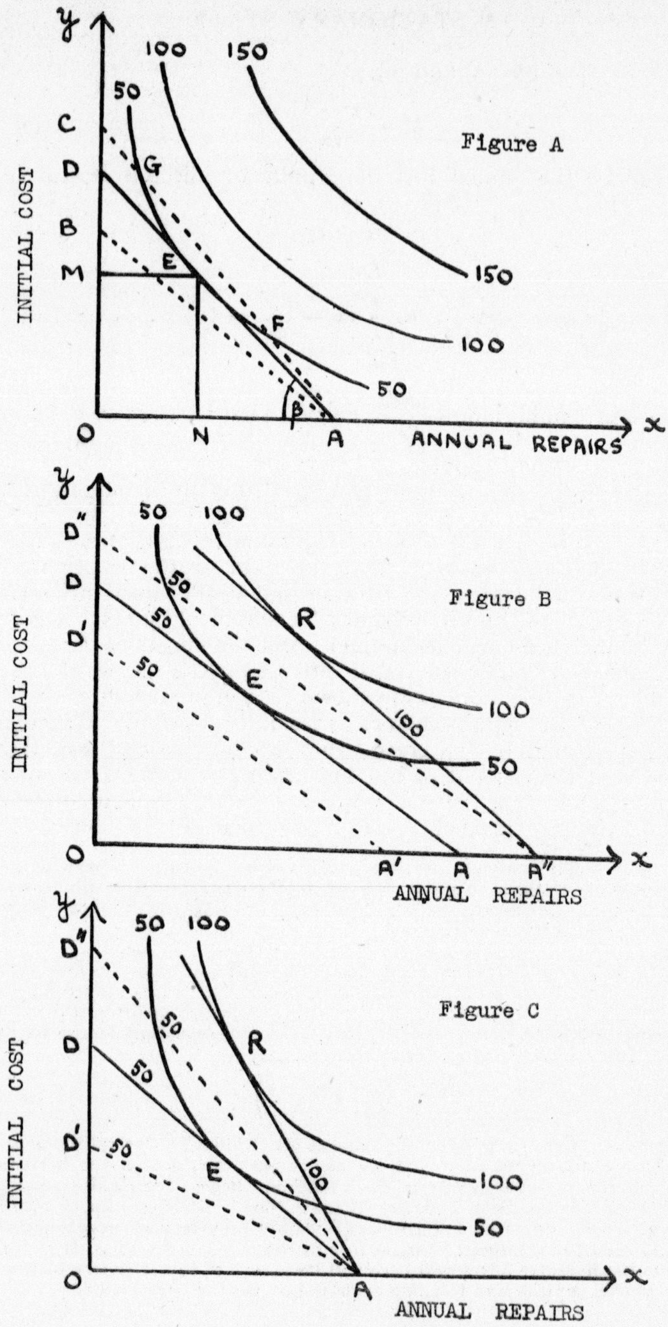
y
100
150
50
C
D
B
M
G
E
F
INITIAL COST
Figure A
150
100
50
β
O
N
A
ANNUAL REPAIRS
x
y
50
100
D"
D
D'
50
50
50
Figure B
R
E
100
100
50
INITIAL COST
O
A'
A
A"
x
ANNUAL REPAIRS
y
50
100
D"
D
D'
50
50
50
Figure C
R
E
100
100
50
INITIAL COST
O
A
x
ANNUAL REPAIRS

Figure 1

curve numbered 50 represents the various combinations of initial cost and annual repair expenditure which together give a length of life of 50 years. The other two curves represent combinations which make the length of life 100 years and 150 years respectively. We must imagine an infinite number of such indifference curves lying between those actually drawn; for, by adding small enough amounts of building activity to either co-ordinate, we can increase the length of life by as small an amount as we please. Something can be said about the shape of these curves. They do not cross; it is impossible to get two lengths of life with the same combination of initial cost and repair expenditure. They slope downwards; if we add to the initial cost we must decrease the repair expenditure in order to stay on the same length-of-life indifference curve and vice versa. Finally, as in Figure 1, they are *convex* to the origin; for, as initial cost is diminished, more and more units of building activity have to be expended annually in repairs in order to keep the house on the same length-of-life indifference curve, and vice versa. The slope of the curve at any point, such as E, represents the amount of initial cost which is required to compensate for a loss of a small unit of annual expenditure on repairs in order that the building may retain the same length of life [1]; this becomes steeper and steeper as A approaches the origin.

Let us assume that the community (or individual) has a certain income which, at the existing cost of building activity, would enable him to buy OA units of building activity per annum. Now, if we know the rate of interest *and* the length of life of the building, we know the amount of initial building activity which can be exchanged for one unit of annual repair building activity (the latter must equal the annual interest payment plus the annual amortisation quota). Using our previous notation, it is $\frac{(\alpha - 1)}{i\alpha}$ units of initial cost. If we draw a line through A at an angle β such that

$$\tan \beta = -\frac{(\alpha - 1)}{i\alpha},$$

points on this line represent alternative combinations of initial cost and annual repair cost which can be purchased with the income OA at the existing rate of interest and with the particular length of life; the slope of the line is the annual price of initial cost. Since $\tan \beta = -\frac{1}{i}\left(1 - \frac{1}{\alpha}\right)$, it increases numerically as α increases. But α varies directly with L, therefore it follows that as L increases the slope of this "opportunity line" increases.

[1] It is, therefore, the rate of substitution k of initial cost for annual repair cost.

Let us assume that the rate of interest is given. Then for any length of life we can draw *one* indifference curve and *one* " opportunity line " only. In Figure A three possible " opportunity lines " (say, on the basis of three different rates of interest) are considered with a given length-of-life indifference curve (50 years). *AB* is the case where the line does not reach the length-of-life indifference curve. In that case it is impossible to purchase sufficient building activity to construct such a house with the existing income *OA*. *AC* is the case where the line cuts the length-of-life indifference curve. In that case it is possible to build a house with a life of 50 years by occupying position *F* or position *G*. But at the point *F* the slope of the indifference curve is less than the slope of the " opportunity line ", and by buying initial cost with repairs it is possible to obtain *more* than the initial cost required to remain on the 50 years indifference curve. Thus the length of life in this case can be made greater than 50 years. Similarly at the point *G* it pays to substitute repairs for initial cost in order once again to increase the length of life above 50 years. The case of the " opportunity line " cutting the indifference curve thus means that a higher length of life may be obtained with the same income. Finally, *AD* is the case where the " opportunity line " *touches* the indifference curve at *E*. In this case the slope of the indifference curve at *E* (the rate of substitution of initial cost for annual repair expenditure) is the same as the slope of the " opportunity line " (the price in terms of repairs of an additional unit of initial cost). This means that, at this point *E*, by purchasing initial cost with repairs, or vice versa, no addition can be made to the length of life of the house; equilibrium is attained. This is obviously the same condition of equilibrium as equation (8) since the slope of the curve is k and the slope of the " opportunity line " is $\frac{(\alpha - 1)}{i\alpha}$.

It is now easy to see how equilibrium is established. Starting with a low length of life, where the " opportunity line " *cuts* the indifference curve, the length of life is increased until a value is found where the " opportunity line " *touches* its indifference curve. When this happens the maximum length of life has been determined. At the same time the amounts of initial cost (*e.g. OM*) and annual repairs (*e.g. ON*) are also determined by the point of equilibrium.

What happens when, with a given income, the cost of building activity changes? This situation is shown in Figure B of Figure 1. Let us suppose that the original equilibrium was at *E*. Since the cost of building activity does not enter into the expression for tan β, the slopes of the " opportunity lines " are unaffected. But the result of a change in the cost of building activity is to shift the lines bodily to the right, *e.g.* $A''D''$, when building costs decrease and to the left, *e.g.* $A'D'$, when building costs increase, the line still being parallel to the line AD. Let us take the case of a decrease in building costs (exactly opposite results hold for an increase). The " opportunity lines " are numbered according to the length of life used in their determination. The new line $A''D''$ *cuts* the indifference curve for 50 years, so that the result of the fall in building costs must be an *increase* in the length of life of the buildings. As the length of life is increased the slope of the " opportunity line " increases until finally a length of life is found such that the " opportunity line " $A''R$ touches the corresponding indifference curve for, say, 100 years. It cannot be determined, unless we know the shape of the indifference curves, how capital cost and repair cost will change. All we can say is that both will not decrease together.

Finally let us examine the case of a change in the interest rate. This is shown on Figure C of Figure 1. Let us suppose that the previous equilibrium has been at the point E. What happens to the line AD when the rate of interest alters? Take the case of a fall in the rate of interest. There are two opposing factors: on the one hand the annual interest charge will decline, but on the other hand the amortisation charge will rise (a point often overlooked when considering the effects of changes in the interest rate on investment). Which of these factors has the greater effect? Differentiating the numerical value of tan β with respect to i we find that it is negative if

$$\left(1 + \frac{1}{i}\right)(\alpha - 1) > (L + 1)$$

which, if we neglect powers of i becomes

$$(1 + i)(L + 1) > (L + 1)$$

and is obviously true. This means that as long as there is any rate of interest at all a rise in the rate of interest decreases the slope of the " opportunity line " and it turns to AD' while a fall in the rate of interest increases the slope of the " opportunity line " and it turns to AD''. Let us assume that it rises to AD''. Then, since this new line *cuts* the indifference curve, the length of life will *increase*. The rise in the length of life further increases the slope of the line until a length of life is discovered of, say, 100 years for which the " opportunity line " AR touches the indifference curve at R. We cannot, however, say definitely whether the capital cost or repair expenditure or both will increase; that depends upon the shape of the curves.

The effect of a fall in building costs or in the rate of interest on total building activity depends on the influence of the new values of u, v, and L upon x as expressed in equation (1). When the indifference curves are in the form of rectangular hyperbolas both u and v will increase, L will increase, and the effect on building activity depends on whether $\frac{mu}{L}$ increases and, if it does not, whether mv increases more than $\frac{mu}{L}$ decreases.

Throughout this analysis we suppose, of course, that the total annual expenditure on the buildings is fixed. We are quite justified in doing so if we assume that there are no changes in incomes and tastes; for we have implicitly assumed that equilibrium exists when this fixed annual sum is expended on these buildings (standard in quality, size and type, but variable in durability).

CHAPTER III

A DYNAMIC ECONOMY: DEMOGRAPHIC FACTORS

1. INTRODUCTION

THE considerations of the last chapter apply to an economy in which the very special conditions outlined in the assumptions exist. The assumptions which had to be made are obviously very rigid and highly unreal; but merely to set up the conditions of such an economy has been useful for the purpose of revealing the complexity of the forces which operate on building activity in the real world. We can now proceed to relax our assumptions one by one. In the present chapter we consider the effects of changing demographic factors.

2. THE NUMBER OF FAMILIES

Passing from a stationary economy, in which houses are all alike and the number of families, average size of the family, and ratio of families to dwellings are constant, we now examine what are the consequences of changes in *the number of families* upon the number of houses required, and therefore upon building activity, if all other relevant factors remain unchanged. Before we consider the effects of such changes in detail, it must be pointed out that, from the point of view of building activity, two important factors are operative in the real world which are very relevant to the problem. These factors are (i) the number of families per house, and (ii) the age and sex distribution and marital condition of the population. For the time being it is assumed that the number of families per house remains constant and equal to unity. We will also assume that the age and sex distribution and marital condition of the population remain constant.

We have here the problem of a change, from year to year, in the requirements of the community for family accommodations of a standard size. In the case of an increasing number of families we can distinguish two effects; first, assuming each year that houses for the new families are built within the year,[1] there will be an expenditure of building activity simply to provide the new houses, and secondly, as time goes on the number of houses requiring annual repairs and the number of houses falling to be replaced each year, assuming a constant length of life, will steadily increase as the number of families, and hence the number of houses, increases. In the case of a decreasing number of families, the situation becomes more complicated. In this case the precise result depends upon the relative sizes of the annual replacement quota for existing houses and the number of families by which the total number of families is decreasing annually.

This analysis can, however, be connected conveniently with our analysis on pp. 22 to 36. Consider the stationary economy of the last chapter, where

m = Number of families;
L = Length of life of houses;
u = Initial cost in units of building acitivity;
v = Annual repairs in units of building activity.

The annual building activity is $\frac{mu}{L} + mv$ units. What is the effect of an increase or decrease in the number of families? Let the ratio of u to v be σ, a constant, *i.e.*, $u = \sigma v$; in general σ is a large number, for repairs are usually small compared with replacement cost. This is an extremely artificial assumption since the ratio of u to v varies greatly from house to house and from year to year, but the assumption simplifies the analysis without affecting the results.

The annual building activity x_1, before the increase in families, would be,

$$x_1 = \frac{mu}{L} + mv = mu\left(\frac{1}{L} + \frac{1}{\sigma}\right) \text{ units} \quad . \quad . \quad . \quad . \quad (10)$$

Now an increase or decrease in the number of families

[1] *I.e.* that a housing standard of one family per house is always maintained.

can be either (*a*) a *single* increase or decrease of m_1 from m to $(m \pm m_1)$ in one year without any further changes in the number of families, or (*b*) *yearly* increases or decreases, $m_1, m_2, m_3, \ldots$ etc. In the case of an increase in any one year of m_t families the additional accommodations required are m_t houses, and there are two possible methods of supplying them. Either all the houses can be provided in one year or the building can be spread over several years. And the effect on building activity will depend upon the length of time, say n years, over which the building is distributed. In the case of a decrease, the length of time over which the drop in building is distributed will depend upon the ratio of m_t to the replacement quota $\frac{m}{L}$, and n will equal $m_t L/m$. Variations in the yearly increases or decreases $m_1, m_2, m_3 \ldots$, etc., will, of course, lead to corresponding variations in building activity unless n is allowed to vary as m_t. It is also apparent that any variations in new building as a result of the changes in number of families will affect building activity in years to come when the houses fall to be replaced, and increases in families may thus lead to cycles of construction. In addition to the change in new construction, there is also an addition to or subtraction from the number of houses and hence to the amount of annual repairs required.

The change in building activity in the first year is either $m_t u$ or $\frac{m_t u}{n}$ according to whether the new building is immediately executed or spread over n years, and the proportionate change in building activity is found by comparing this change with $mu\left(\frac{1}{L} + \frac{1}{\sigma}\right)$. The following table shows how the proportionate change in building activity depends upon the ratio of u to v (here called σ), the length of life of the building L and the value of n. Numerical values of the constants are inserted to illustrate the magnitude of the effects of population changes.

This table clearly brings out the powerful influence on building activity of a change in the number of families when the adjustment is made rapidly and the extent to which it is modified when the building is spread over time. If we assumed empty houses to exist, more than one family to occupy a dwelling, and the length of life of houses and the number of families per dwelling to vary according to pressure on accommodation, factors which are definitely operative in the real world, the effects of an increase or decrease in

Annual Change in Building Activity Due to a Change in the Number of Families.

Value of *n*.	Change in Building Activity as a Ratio of Former Building Activity.	% Change in Building Activity due to 1% Change in Number of Families.	
		$L = 75$. $\sigma = 100$.	$L = 50$. $\sigma = 50$.
$n = 1$	$\frac{m_t}{m} \cdot \frac{\sigma L}{(\sigma + L)n}$	43%	25%
$n = 10$	$\frac{m_t}{10m} \cdot \frac{\sigma L}{(\sigma + L)n}$	4·3%	2·5%

population would, of course, be modified. We can conclude, however, that changes in the number of families are extremely important factors in determining the annual building activity and that, in general, movements of the total number of families result in greatly magnified movements of building activity.

Having analysed the consequences which follow an increase or decrease in the number of families in an area (assuming the size of the family to be constant and the number of families per dwelling to be unity), we see that population changes bringing about continuous, though varying, changes in the number of families, are likely in general to cause continued, though varying, annual changes in building activity which are likely to be repeated in cycles with a period equal to the lifetime of a house.

3. Size of Family, Age and Sex Distribution, and Marital Condition

The natural procedure which one would adopt, and which is usually adopted when dealing with population movements, is to consider changes in total population and in the average size of family. But such a classification is unsuitable for our purpose. Since a population has characteristics of age, sex, and marital condition, and since "average size of family" conceals the distribution of families by size, and age and sex composition, the "size of the population" and "average size of family" hide more than they reveal. However, the size of the population divided by the average size of family gives us the total number of families in the population which, as we have seen, is most important in determining building activity, since it determines the number of family accommodations required once the housing standard is given. The change in the number of families is, of course, related to the change in the size of the population and the average size of the family, and in most cases changes in the size of the total population involve changes in age and sex distribution and marital condition. We now consider what modifications to our previous analysis arise when we drop the assumptions of constant size of family, constant age and sex distribution and constant marital condition. In other words, what effects on building activity in addition to those of the changing *number* of families are caused by changes in these variables?

We can make a general analysis of a simultaneous change in number of families, average size of family, age and sex distribution, and marital condition by considering what changes will cause the removal of a family from one house to another. The problem is, of course, closely related with family incomes and the forces which determine the amount of family income which can be spent on rent. A change in the size of a family and its age and sex composition may cause a change in family income and a consequent change in the amount which is spent on rent. But families seldom change their accommodation on the grounds of changes in size alone; income changes would seem to be far more important except, perhaps, in the higher income groups. Even when a family takes in a boarder or lodger the reason is seldom that the dwelling is considered too large, but rather that an addition to the family income is required. Our conclusion concerning the influence of changes in size of family and age and sex composition of the family, when economic factors are constant, must be, therefore, that no additional building of houses will be generated in excess of normal replacement; but the houses built to replace those falling derelict will, of course, be of a type suitable for the new type of family. Superimposed upon the effects of the changing size of family will be the effects of changes in the *number* of families which have already been considered, and changes in family incomes which will be considered later.

Changes in age and sex distribution and marital condition have an influence upon building activity only through their effect on the number of families. The influence of age and sex composition upon building activity arises through their effect on the number of bachelors, spinisters, and unattached elderly persons who form the bulk of the single person families. Changes in marital condition such as, for instance, a later age at marriage will also operate in the same way by affecting the number of single person families. The additional effects of these variables are very slight, since they can be reduced to those of a changing number of families which have already been analysed. They may be mitigated by compensating changes in such factors as the number of unoccupied houses, the length of life of houses, number of families per dwelling, and economic factors.

4. Spatial Movements of Population

Spatial movements of population may be of three types

(1) Migration internationally, *i.e.* movements of population to or from a national area;

(2) Migration from one part of a country to another,

owing to variations in economic conditions between areas within the country, and in particular to shifting of industries;

(3) Migration from town to country, or vice versa, within a small area, *i.e.* movements due to changes in habits, customs, and tastes, combined with changes in incomes and prices.

Since we are considering building activity in one national area alone, movements of the first type can be neglected. They can be included in the same category as any other influences which act upon the size of the population. Movements of the second and third types are, however, entirely within the national area, and their effects upon building activity need to be considered. Because of the post-war increase in internal migration in this country and the tendency of the population to be "country minded", these two types of movement have been very important in determining the extent of residential building. The cheapening of transport and the vast growth of building societies, with their large-scale advertising of the advantages of the suburbs, have already helped to bring about such movements on a gigantic scale, and fears of air-raids are likely to have a similar result.

Spatial movements of population will have very important influences on building activity through their obvious effects on the populations of the areas affected. When population moves from area A to area B there is a sudden increase in the population of B and a sudden decrease in the population of A. Assuming that, initially, there were exactly sufficient houses to accommodate the population in both areas, this clearly results in a surplus of houses in area A and a shortage of houses in area B, simply because houses cannot be moved from one area to another. The effects of spatial movements on the separate areas are, therefore, analogous to those effects of changes in the number of families already examined. But the effects are likely to be far more intense since natural movements in the size of the population are limited, while spatial movements often amount to as much as 2·5% per annum.[1] There is an important consideration to be borne in mind, however, in the fact that, for the country as a whole, the influence on total building activity will be less than the effects on either of the two areas separately, since the effects in the losing will tend to neutralise the effects in the gaining area.

The effect upon total building activity in the whole country depends upon the relation between the number of families moving from area A to area B (say N) and the "replacement quota" in area A (say R). N may be greater than, equal to, or less than R. If N is less than or equal to R, then the increase in building activity in the gaining area B can be exactly offset by the decrease in building activity in area A, since the excess houses in A will not be replaced. In general, spatial movements are on such a large scale and the length of life of buildings is so long that N is many times greater than R; in that case there is an increase in total building activity in the whole country by an amount sufficient for the building of $(N - R)$ houses. The net effect upon total building activity is, therefore, usually very intense.

For purposes of analysing the effects of spatial movements of population on building activity, the moving population can be separated into whole families (married persons with or without children, and single person families) and parts of families splitting off from existing families (spinsters, bachelors, widows and widowers). Whole families will demand, if income permits, a structurally separate dwelling of their own. On the other hand, parts of families are likely either to join up with other families or to form separate single-person families on their own. Finally, if the parts of families are in those age-groups in which marriage usually takes place and migration occurs among both sexes, the net addition to the number of families in the receiving area will ultimately be still further reduced. The actual effect depends also upon the age, sex, and marital composition

[1] The average migration from Glamorgan was 2·44% per annum from July 1927 to June 1931.

of the inflowing population compared with that of the gaining area.

The effects of spatial movements therefore depend upon the age, sex, and marital composition of the moving population, and the ultimate effects, first, upon the number of families in the losing area and, second, upon the number of families in the gaining area. In general, these two effects will not neutralise each other, since the splitting up of families in the losing area will be greater than the re-combination of parts of families in the gaining area and will cause a net addition to the total number of families in the country. Spatial movements are generally associated, therefore, with considerable increases in building activity in the gaining areas, and in the country as a whole.

Another important consideration in the case of internal migration is that it may be permanent or temporary and that its real nature in this respect is usually uncertain. Expectations regarding the permanent or temporary character of the movements will therefore be important influences upon both the quantity and quality of the buildings erected. As with changes in the number of families generally, another important factor is the length of time over which building for new families is extended. In the case of internal movements there is inevitably a substantial lag in the adjustment of the number of family accommodation to the number of families, but once the building commences it soon attains a scale commensurate with the size of the inflowing population, and is therefore very intense.

In the case of temporary movements, such as those of holiday-makers, the effects are similar in direction but not in magnitude to those following permanent movements, although in this case economic factors such as the level of income will be more important in determining the extent and nature of the buildings erected to accommodate such movements.

In addition to the effects of spatial migration upon residential building activity, there will be effects upon factory and commercial building and upon the construction of public works. The inflowing population require not only houses but the great variety of shops, offices, factories and workshops, roads, bridges, and so on, necessary to administer to their needs. Spatial migration is therefore the most important single demographic factor influencing total building activity.

5. "Building Need"

The influence of changes in the number of families on the demand for new residential buildings has been considered by Roos.[1] He crystallised the effects of such changes into a single measurement which he called "building need". We present here a more general form of his measurement.

Before we can measure "building need" we must choose some arbitrary ideal standard of housing of q' families per dwelling, "building need" then being defined as the shortage of houses if the ideal standard is aimed at.

Consider any period of time and let the actual number of families per dwelling at the beginning of the period considered be q. Let the number of families at the beginning of years 1, 2, 3, etc., be m_1, m_2, m_3, etc., and the number of houses built in each year be h_1, h_2, h_3, etc.

The initial "building need" is merely $m_1 \left(\frac{1}{q'} - \frac{1}{q}\right)$, and in each subsequent year we must add the number of houses required for new families (*i.e.* the increase in families divided by q') and subtract the net addition to the number of houses in existence. The increase in families in year s is $m_{s+1} - m_s$, hence the number of houses required for the additional families is $\frac{m_{s+1} - m_s}{q'}$. The net addition to the number of houses in existence in year s is the number of houses built, h_s, minus the number of houses falling to be replaced during the year. In order to allow for these replacements we now introduce the concept of a "replacement rate" for houses. This was defined as "the ratio of dwellings torn down or otherwise destroyed during a year to the number of dwellings at the beginning of the year",[2] and is denoted

[1] C. F. Roos, *Dynamic Economics*, Bloomington, 1934, p. 80.
[2] *Op. cit.*, p. 80.

by r. Let us assume that the replacement rate for the buildings existing at the beginning of the period is constant over the period and equal to r. We neglect the replacement of new buildings, since most new buildings will not require replacement during, say, 10 years, but still assume that houses built 1, 2, 3, or 10 years before the beginning of the period need replacing at a rate r. Our measure cannot therefore be safely applied except over relatively short periods.

At the end of the first year of the period the building need is

$$B_1 = S_1 + N_1 + \frac{F_1}{q'}$$ assuming an ideal standard of q' families per house (or family accommodation)

where B_1 is building need at the end of year 1, S_1 is the initial shortage $m_1\left(\frac{1}{q'} - \frac{1}{q}\right)$, N_1 the replacements required in year 1, and $\frac{F_1}{q'}$ the new houses required for F_1 new families.

In the second year it is

$$B_2 = N_1 + \frac{F_2}{q'}, \text{ and so on}$$

if the initial shortage is now supposed to have been supplied. N_1, the number of houses replaced annually, is a constant here over the whole period and is equal to

$$r \,.\, \frac{m_1}{q}$$

since $\frac{m_1}{q}$ is the number of buildings existing at the beginning of the period, and we are assuming that new houses do not need replacement. Substituting for N_1 and remembering that $F_s = m_{s+1} - m_s$, and summing over a period of n years the building need becomes

$$\sum_{s=1}^{s=n} B_s = S_1 + \frac{nrm_1}{q} + \sum_{s=1}^{s=n} \frac{(m_{s+1} - m_s)}{q'} - \sum_{s=1}^{s=n} h_s$$

$$= m_1\left(\frac{1}{q'} - \frac{1}{q}\right) + \frac{nrm_1}{q} + \frac{(m_n - m_1)}{q'} - \sum_{s=1}^{s=n} h_s \quad (11)$$

where q is the actual and q' is the ideal number of families per dwelling accommodation, and h_s is the number of new houses built in the year s. This formula simply means that the building need is equal to the sum of (*a*) the initial shortage, (*b*) the replacements required for the old buildings over the whole period, and (*c*) the amount of new building required for new families over the whole period, reduced by (*d*) the actual building during the whole period.

If we find the value of q at the beginning of the period, empirically, and choose q', our ideal number of families per dwelling, we have here a measure of " building need " on that basis. This measure takes account of the fact that q is usually greater than unity, and allows for variations in the number of families per dwelling from Census to Census, and is therefore applicable to actual conditions.

There are two main criticisms to be made of this method of treating building need. First, by choosing any standard such as one dwelling per family or q' families per dwelling we are using an average obtained from two essentially heterogeneous quantities—families and dwellings—and treating them as if they were homogeneous. However, since it would be impossible to find any practical system of measurement for this problem in which the units are homogeneous, we must find some standard which gives the nearest approach to homogeneity and at the same time retains practicability. This, we think, would be to consider one family per dwelling as a state of affairs towards which society is tending under the psychological impulses which drive each family to seek at least one structurally separate dwelling accommodation of its own if it possibly can. In our statistical analysis q' will therefore be made equal to one. In that case equation (11) is simplified by introducing N, the number of dwelling accommodations at the beginning of the period, and the equation becomes :

" Building need " at the end of year n

$$= m_1 - N + nrN + (m_n - m_1) - \sum_{s=1}^{s=n} h_s \quad . \quad (12)$$

This method supposes that there is no " undercrowding ",

i.e. that no families inhabit more than one dwelling. In actual fact some families do inhabit more than one dwelling, and our estimates of building need will therefore be too small on this account. However, the number of families in this happy position is at present small enough to be neglected, and any estimates based on (12) will be good approximations.

Secondly, one must note that there has been another important simplifying assumption in this analysis. It has been assumed that every dwelling will satisfy the need of one family. But this neglects all *spatial* considerations : a demand (or need) for a dwelling involves the preference of a certain position in a particular district, and therefore every dwelling will not satisfy this demand. A surplus of houses in Glasgow cannot offset surplus families in London. Thus "building need" cannot be measured for several areas and then found for the whole area by addition. This means that the value obtained for "building need" depends upon the size of the area considered, and if that area is composed of very dissimilar parts, the estimate of "building need" is likely to be a serious underestimate. Finally it should be noticed that "building need" takes no account of the requirements of the community for repairs and alterations.

6. The Measurement of the Replacement Rate

Before we can make estimates of "building need" from our formula, we must calculate the crude replacement rate for family accommodations which appears there as an unknown. This is usually given some arbitrary value when calculating the number of houses required to attain some desired standard of housing, but an accurate calculation, if attainable, would be useful for many purposes. Roos' definition of r given previously is that "the replacement rate is the ratio of dwellings torn down or otherwise destroyed during a year to the number of dwellings at the beginning of the year". This is quite a neat and consistent definition, but is faulty in that a derelict building which is not torn down owing, for instance, to the cost of demolition is excluded. However, this is unavoidable statistically, since derelict family accommodations are not separately enumerated in the Census, and consequently Roos' definition is used.

The replacement rate can best be regarded as a kind of "suicide rate". For, although we may not be able to say exactly when any particular building will be replaced (that depends upon many demographic, economic, and psychological factors), we can say that, out of a large number of buildings, a certain proportion will be replaced annually and that this proportion is not likely to be subject to very violent fluctuations for any given area over a short period of time. Past fluctuations in the rate of building will, however, cause corresponding variations in the number of replacements, though there is, of course, some flexibility in the replacement rate.

Barnes [1] calculated the rate for Manchester, Bradford, Newcastle-upon-Tyne, Leeds, and Sheffield over the years 1901–11. He calculated (i) the number of houses actually built in this period and (ii) the increase in the number of houses from 1901 to 1911. The difference gave him the replacements, and the ratio of the replacements per annum to the houses at the beginning of the decade gave a measure of the annual crude replacement rate. His results were 0·00053, 0·00365, 0·0073, 0·0084, and 0·00512, respectively, for the five towns. The usefulness of these results for such small areas seems very questionable, the fourth rate, for example, being about 16 times that of the first, perhaps owing to the fact that the rate obviously depends upon past fluctuations in the rate of building, *i.e.* upon the age distribution of houses.

One of the principal defects in the foregoing analysis is that the unit on which it is based is a "house". This hides one difficulty we are trying to overcome. A "house" may be a working-class cottage, a large villa, a block of flats, or a tenement, and may contain one or many family dwelling units, and our figures are likely, therefore, to mean quite different things when there is a bias in favour of any particular type. This is likely to be the case in practice,

[1] H. Barnes, *Housing*, p. 361.

since new houses are likely to be of that type for which the demand is higher, and consequently houses demolished may contain quite a different number of family accommodations than do those built to replace them. This seems to indicate that our unit should be "family accommodations", or, to use the modern Census term, "structurally separate dwellings", and that all our units of house-room should be expressed in these terms if they are to have any consistent meaning. In the statistical analysis of demographic factors in Chapter VII we use Barnes' method, but use "structurally separate dwellings" as our unit of house-room; the errors involved in using this measure are, moreover, minimised by applying it only to short periods of ten years.

CHAPTER IV

A DYNAMIC ECONOMY: ECONOMIC FACTORS

BUILDINGS FOR OCCUPATION

1. What are Demand and Supply?

In dealing with problems in the building industry it is easy to arrive at a state of complete confusion over the words "supply" and "demand". There are two reasons for this difficulty. First, that by "demand" is often meant "need", and not, as it should, the quantity of an economic good (which includes services) demanded *at a given price*. Even in chapter III, where we consider "building need", it is easy to confuse "need" with the effective demand for house-room at some given price, or with the whole demand schedule; whereas "building need" is rather the pressure which would, if economic factors allowed, be exerted on the existing accommodation, one of the main factors which determine the demand schedule for house room. By "demand" we should, then, always mean the basis of a demand schedule, that is, the amount demanded at a given price. The second source of confusion is that the term "demand for building" does not adequately define the economic good demanded. In connection with the building industry very different things may be demanded: (*a*) buildings for occupation, (*b*) buildings for ownership, and (*c*) building activity. Unless we rigidly separate these demand schedules, we shall never solve our problems satisfactorily. Even this necessary distinction is a little confusing, since "buildings for occupation", "buildings for ownership", and "building activity" are not homogeneous units like pounds of butter or loaves of bread and, in reality, must be separated into such arbitrary divisions as working-class houses, middle-class houses, factories, shops, etc., or bricklaying, painting, new building, repairs and alterations. However, we can, for simplicity, consider the three broad divisions: demand for buildings for occupation, demand for buildings for ownership, and demand for building activity. Analogous considerations apply to the word "supply", and once more the same three divisions may be considered.

We have, therefore, the following markets:

(*a*) The supply of and demand for buildings for occupation, which determine the level of rents;

(*b*) The supply of and demand for buildings for ownership, which determine the level of prices of buildings; and

(*c*) The supply of and demand for building activity, which determine the level of building costs.

The Characteristics of a Building

It is useful, before analysing the three divisions above, to consider briefly what are the characteristics of a building. They are

(i) *Geographical position*, which brings to mind problems of town versus country, of population movements, and of local amenities and environment.

(ii) *Size of building*, which brings up problems of adaptation of buildings to families, size of families, number of families per dwelling, capacity of factories, warehouses, shops, and so on.

(iii) *Technical design*, which depends upon technical knowledge of materials and methods of construction, and upon fashion; it has important effects upon costs of building and length of life.

(iv) *Quality and kinds of materials*, which depend upon inventions, tastes, and availability of materials. These determine the physical properties of the building, such as its heating, lighting, and acoustic properties; its probable physical length of life and the annual repairs required.

(v) *Substitutability*. An important consideration is the fact that, by expending building activity upon an existing building, its size, technical design, and quality can be changed considerably and this may render a new building unnecessary, particularly when geographical position is a minor factor.

It is plain that there are infinite variations in these characteristics, and for this reason every house is, strictly speaking, different from any other, although in some areas the variation is only slight. This is a very important factor, and should be borne in mind throughout the whole of our study of demand for and supply of buildings.

We can, to a large extent, overcome the difficulties which arise through this heterogeneity by placing buildings into different rental classes within which the buildings are let at approximately the same rent. There can, of course, be no hard-and-fast division on this basis, particularly for factory and commercial buildings, but by using this device we can make a close approach to reality. In the case of factory and commercial buildings, the buildings being more specific would need to be further sub-divided into homogeneous groups classified according to the industries for which the building might be suitable. Assuming that all buildings fall into such rental classes it is important to note that, by expending different amounts of building activity on repairs and alterations, any particular building can be shifted into any one of a limited range of different rental classes (and different industries in the case of factory and commercial buildings).

If this sub-division into rental classes is made, we obtain not one level of rent but a whole complex of rents for different rental classes, and not one level of prices of buildings but a complex of prices of buildings. Similarly we can sub-divide building activity into different trades and we get, not a single level of costs, but a complex of costs for brickwork, joinery, plastering, painting, and so on. We can, however, define a unit of building activity as a combination of the services of the various workers in the building industry with the various materials used in building, all being combined in some fixed proportion. We obtain, therefore, one single measure of building costs—the cost of one unit of building activity.

In this chapter (and in Chapter V) we require some method of analysing the economic phenomena connected with the building industry in a manner which will cover the whole set of phenomena and yet leave the minimum amount of overlapping of divisions. It is impossible to devise a logical division for the building industry where no overlapping will occur, but the best possible division seems to be the following.

A. *Demand for Buildings for Occupation.*

- (i) Residential,
- (ii) Factory and Commercial,
  - (*a*) Rent-payer;
  - (*b*) Owner-occupier;
  - (*c*) Municipalities and Government;
- (iii) Public Works and Miscellaneous (Government and other bodies).

B. *Supply of Buildings for Occupation.*

- (i) Residential,
- (ii) Factory and Commercial,
  - (*a*) Owner-occupier;
  - (*b*) Investor [1];
  - (*c*) Speculative builder;
  - (*d*) Municipalities and Government;
- (iii) Public Works and Miscellaneous (Government and other bodies).

C. *Demand for Buildings for Ownership.*

- (i) Residential,
- (ii) Factory and Commercial,
  - (*a*) Owner-occupier;
  - (*b*) Investor;
  - (*c*) Municipalities and Government;
- (iii) Public Works and Miscellaneous (Government and other bodies).

D. *Supply of Buildings for Ownership.*

- (i) Residential,
- (ii) Factory and Commercial,
  - (*a*) Owner-occupier;
  - (*b*) Investor;
  - (*c*) Speculative builder;
  - (*d*) Municipalities and Government;
- (iii) Public Works and Miscellaneous (Government and other bodies).

[1] The "investor" is defined as a person who purchases a house as an investment and not for his own use.

E. *Demand for Building Activity.*

(1) *New Buildings:*

(i) Residential,
(ii) Factory and Commercial,
- (*a*) Owner-occupier;
- (*b*) Investor;
- (*c*) Speculative builder;
- (*d*) Municipalities and Government;

(iii) Public Works and Miscellaneous (Government and other bodies).

(2) *Demolition* (a, b, c, d above).
(3) *Repairs and alterations* (a, b, c, d above and, sometimes, the rent-payer).

F. *Supply of Building Activity.*

(*a*) The building and public-works contractors;
(*b*) The jobbing builders, painters, and decorators;
(*c*) The speculative builders.

One important fact emerges from this division. The sections under " demand for building activity " and " supply of buildings for ownership " are found to contain the same persons. As soon as one considers this fact, light is thrown on the whole problem; for it is obvious that there is a very close link between the *demand* for building activity and the *supply* of buildings for ownership. *The* effective *demand for a large section of building activity becomes, after a time lag, the supply of buildings for ownership.* But in spite of their connection, it is essential always to keep the two divisions and their particular problems separate and distinct.

Furthermore, the sections " demand for buildings for ownership " and " supply of buildings for occupation " are also found to contain the same persons. This brings out the important fact that *the* effective *demand for buildings for ownership becomes the supply of buildings for occupation.* Once again, however, we must, as far as possible, keep them separate.

It also becomes obvious, from the above scheme, that the same persons, *e.g.* the owner-occupier and the speculative builder, may appear in different categories; in these cases the individuals perform two functions simultaneously, that is, they supply to satisfy their own demand. The owner-occupier supplies for occupation to satisfy his own demand; the speculative builder supplies building activity and supplies buildings for ownership. This also brings out the important fact that rents, prices of buildings, and costs, being determined by their appropriate supply and demand schedules, are connected in some way through the individuals concerned. But this problem must be deferred until the next chapter.

A distinction must be made between "potential" and "actual" demand for or supply of buildings (for occupation and ownership) and building activity. This is extremely important, since it brings out clearly that we are thinking in terms of demand and supply schedules. At any given price there is an actual *effective* demand, while there are *potential* demands at other prices. In the case of the owner-occupier, for instance, we have to realise that he is *effectively* demanding his own house for occupation and supplying it for occupation at the same time. Again, he is *effectively* demanding his own house for ownership and supplying it for ownership to himself. But, under favourable conditions, he *may* supply the building for occupation to another person and demand another building for occupation himself, without necessarily demanding the second for ownership, or he *may* supply the building for ownership to some other person who is demanding for ownership, and these are *potentialities* which depend upon the level of rents and prices of buildings. In the subsequent analysis each of the respective types is introduced by explaining, first, in which schedules he *actually* appears, and, secondly, in which schedules he is most likely to appear *potentially*. Every person, of course, demands some accommodation for himself for occupation, but it is less confusing if we ignore this aspect of economic life in the case of such persons as the investor in houses when other aspects are our primary concern.

The object of this chapter is to consider the factors involved in the equilibrium between demand for and supply of buildings for occupation. The market for buildings for ownership and the market for building activity will be analysed separately in the next chapter.

2. Buildings for Occupation: Demand

(a) *Residential Buildings*

The Rent-payer and Owner-occupier.

The rent-payer and owner-occupier are considered together because each demands for occupation and each must expend a certain weekly cost in return for a certain subjective income. In the case of the rent-payer the cost is his weekly rent, and in the case of the owner-occupier the cost is the cost of the capital outlay plus maintenance and repair expenditure.

The rent-payer actually demands for occupation. Since he may in favourable circumstances become an owner-occupier, he potentially demands for ownership, supplies for ownership, and supplies for occupation. Since he may have a house built, he potentially demands building activity. The owner-occupier actually supplies to satisfy his own demand for occupation, and for ownership; if he ever lets his house, he supplies for occupation to others.

The demand for residential buildings for occupation is very complex, since, as we have seen, residential buildings are of many styles, sizes, geographical positions, and qualities. However, if we consider any single family and its demands for house-room, the essential problem is to relate the marginal utility of "house-room",[1] with the marginal utility of the money cost of house-room (which for existing families includes the cost of using it and an allowance for the money and subjective cost of removals). Obviously a very important factor in determining these marginal utilities is the amount of the family income which can be spent on rent. This, and therefore the demand for occupation, depends upon the size of the family income; its tastes; the size of the family, which dictates the size of accommodation ideally required as well as the expenditure on food and clothing; the cost of living apart from rent; the general level of rent including rates; and expectations of changes in all these variables. A very important item among those entering into the family budget is the cost of transport.

[1] In this context "house-room" must include the attributes—size, quality, style, and position (including amenities).

This is correlated with rent, since in general the greater the distance from an industrial centre the lower is the rent; the level of rent and travelling expenses are therefore considered together as one factor.[1] When all these factors are given for all families the demand schedules for houses for occupation in all rental classes in all areas are determined.

(b) *Factory and Commercial Buildings*

In this case the rent-payer is not so important as the owner-occupier, since very few factories are rented and a large proportion of commercial buildings (shops, offices, warehouses, etc.) are owned by the occupiers. Both the rent-payer and owner-occupier actually demand factory and commercial buildings for occupation; the majority of them are owner-occupiers and actually supply to satisfy their own demand for buildings for occupation and for ownership. This means that we cannot avoid a certain amount of overlapping in our treatment of demand (and supply) for occupation and demand (and supply) for ownership in this section.

Geographical situation, in this instance, is most important since it is necessary to have a factory, shop, warehouse, or office, in that position which gives the lowest combination of costs of production, for the entrepreneur must consider transport facilities, proximity to markets, labour, and power supply, etc. The demand for factory and commercial buildings for occupation in the whole economy is determined by the expansion and contraction of individual firms throughout the whole economy and by

[1] A simple expression which takes all these factors into account in a linear manner yet allows for the fact that larger families have, on the one hand, an increased need for accommodation and, on the other hand, an increased need for food and clothing is,

$$z = a_0 + I\left(a_1 n + \frac{a_2}{P \, . \, n} + a_3 \, . \, \frac{R}{P}\right)$$

where z = family expenditure on rent (including rates) and transport, a_0 = cost of minimum accommodation, I = family income, n = number of equivalent adults, P = cost of living apart from rent, R = level of rents, and a_1, a_2, and a_3 are constants. Unfortunately, simultaneous values of these variables for working-class families are unobtainable, and it has not been possible, therefore, to measure statistically the relative importance of the various factors.

the rate at which firms are coming into and going out of existence. The rate at which firms are being formed or are expanding and the rate at which firms are going out of existence or contracting are influenced by certain common factors. The main factor is obviously profits. If high profits are being made or are expected a firm will expand, maybe after a time lag, and new firms will be formed; when profits are decreasing, firms will go out of existence (or reduce capacity).

A good indication of changes in the possibilities of making profits, and therefore in the desire for increased productive capacity in the whole of industry, is the change in business activity, and we should normally expect an increase in business activity to lead to an increase in factory and commercial building and vice versa. The exact relation between the amount of building and the increase in business activity will, of course, depend upon the initial situation with respect to excess capacity. It will also depend upon the number of vacant factories in existence. In some cases it may only be profitable to embark on production if an existing vacant factory or commercial building is bought or rented, either because of the need for a good position for power and labour supply, transport costs, and so on, or because of the lower capital costs incurred through using an existing factory or commercial building or both. An important factor in this respect is the fact that buildings, particularly factories, are very specific and can only be adapted for different uses by carrying out alterations, and thereby incurring additional cost. Whether it is preferable to use an existing factory or commercial building or not depends, however, on prices of new factories, on the demand for and supply of vacant factories and commercial buildings for occupation, and on costs of alterations. A serious disadvantage of any national index of business activity as an indication of the demand for factory and commercial buildings for occupation is that it does not take account of migration of industry within the country, a factor which is just as important here as the movement of population is to the national demand for residential buildings for occupation.

The annual cost of the building is another factor in determining possible profits and hence the amount of factory and commercial building. This depends upon the level of building costs, the long-term rate of interest, and the level of ground rents and local rates.

The levels of these variables (business activity, building costs, the long-term rate of interest, ground rents, and rates) in different areas at any time will determine the demand schedules for factory and commercial buildings for occupation in all rental classes in all industries.

(c) *Public Works and Miscellaneous*

The Government and other bodies actually demand buildings for occupation and for ownership. In the majority of cases they supply the buildings for occupation and ownership which they themselves demand; they rarely rent their buildings. They demand building activity for new buildings and repairs, and though in some cases they again supply to meet their own demand, the building and public works contractors usually supply the building activity. These persons enter into many schedules, but the following brief analysis of the factors involved in their demand schedule for occupation will suffice also for their supply for occupation, their demand and supply for ownership, and their demand for building activity. Consequently this will be the only mention of "Public Works and Miscellaneous" in the analysis. Public works are undertaken not for profit but for political reasons, *e.g.* to relieve unemployment, or as a part of a plan to stimulate economic activity. Public works cannot be related to economic factors alone. Only one economic factor can be considered really influential, and even this is now of decreasing importance. That factor is the rate of interest on bonds; the best time for corporations to undertake public works is when loans can be raised cheaply, *i.e.*, when the rate of interest is low. Therefore, if we abstract entirely from political factors, the rate of interest (or, of course, the extent of new issues by local authorities) may be regarded as an index of their demand for buildings for occupation and for building activity devoted to public works.

Miscellaneous building (*i.e.*, hospitals, institutions, societies, etc.) not coming under any of these categories is probably also connected with general prosperity, as indicated by an index of business activity. It is not sufficiently important to justify separate treatment in this study.

3. Buildings for Occupation: Supply

(a) *Residential Buildings*

The Owner-occupier.

The owner-occupier supplies to satisfy his own demand for buildings for occupation and ownership. At the same time he is potentially supplying buildings for ownership to others, since, if rents and prices are suitable, he will sell his house and become a rent-payer. Similarly, under favourable conditions, he may let his house for occupation and become a rent-payer in another house. What factors operate to cause a rent-payer to become an owner-occupier and vice versa? First, there are financial factors. The person who wishes to buy a house for his own occupation can do so in the following ways:

(*a*) He can purchase the house outright with cash;

(*b*) He can raise a mortgage on a certain proportion of the value and put down the rest in cash; the mortgage may be raised from trustees, etc., or from local authorities and may or may not be paid off annually;

(*c*) A special case of (*b*)—he can purchase the house through a building society.

In all three cases the new owner-occupier ceases to pay house-rent but commences to pay for repairs and to pay annually for the capital cost of the house.[1] It is the latter item which distinguishes the three cases. In the first case there is an " opportunity-cost " to the owner-occupier, since the money invested in the house could have been invested elsewhere to yield annual dividends. In the second case

[1] Rates, of course, are the same whether the person is a rent-payer or an owner-occupier.

mortgage interest is payable each year on the mortgage, and in addition there is an "opportunity-cost" in respect of the cash deposit. Any repayments of principal will also appear as costs. In the third case there are the same costs as in the second: annual interest charges plus an addition for yearly payments to the sinking fund. In all three cases the actual cost depends upon the cost of the house and upon the level of the long-term rate of interest. In the case of purchase through a building society, by far the most common to-day, the size of the annual payment depends upon the length of time agreed upon to pay off the loan, the proportion of the total cost borrowed, and the long-term rate of interest. The rate of interest charged by the society and the proportion of the total cost advanced depend in turn upon the general level of interest rates, the extent of funds deposited with the society, the demand for these funds, and the policy of the society or association of societies.

There are also non-financial factors at work—namely, the great joy, possibly temporary, which some working-class and middle-class families experience in living in their own houses, the liability attaching to ownership, facilities offered by building societies, and in many cases the desire to be compelled to save.

Expectations of changes in local rates,[1] costs of building and repairs, rents, the rate of interest, and so on, will play a very important rôle in determining the decision of the rent-payer to buy his own house.

The exact influence of the owner-occupier on the supply of buildings for occupation depends, of course, upon the kind of house he buys. If he buys an old house, the results depend upon the actions of the individual who sells. If he builds, he increases the number of buildings in existence and therefore the supply of buildings for occupation. If he buys a new house already built, *e.g.* by a speculative builder, he again influences the supply of buildings for occupation. In general, owner-occupiers prefer *new* houses,

[1] It is, unfortunately, only too true that some local authorities have a habit of raising rateable values a few years after houses have been built, with the result that most new owner-occupiers are faced with unexpectedly high rates.

and an increase in the number of owner-occupiers is therefore accompanied by an increase in the number of houses for occupation, which, of course, inevitably entails an increase in building activity.

The Investor.

Both the owner-occupier and the investor are, fundamentally, investing in houses, but an arbitrary separation has been made here because the motives inducing the investor with spare capital to invest in a house are quite different in many respects from the motives influencing the renter to buy his own house, and therefore involve a different set of factors. In this section we will consider the investor alone.

The investor in houses may be regarded as satisfying his own demand for ownership. He is effectively supplying houses for occupation when he continues to own a house and let it. He effectively supplies houses for ownership when he decides to sell his property, and is therefore always a potential supplier for ownership. If the house he offers for sale has been vacated by the old tenant, he effectively withdraws the house, temporarily, from the supply for occupation. An important point is that when he demands a house for ownership he supplies a house for occupation, and therefore we shall be considering in this section both the demand for ownership and the supply of houses for occupation.

A building is bought as an investment either with the intention of retaining it permanently as a source of income, or with the intention of selling it after some period of time. The original intentions may, of course, be modified in the course of time. We are concerned here, however, with the factors influencing the original decision to buy, since it is the aggregate of individuals' decisions in the present which determine the supply and demand for buildings for occupation and ownership, and the supply and demand for building activity, at any one time.

When a building is bought as a permanent investment the buyer considers the series of rentals (net of rates) he can expect to receive during the lifetime of the building, the repairs he expects to undertake, and the expected value of the building and site at the end of its lifetime. He will plan his investments, repairs, and alterations so as to receive the maximum return over the period.

In the other case, when the building is bought for some shorter period of time, the buyer looks mainly at the expected future course of the capital value of the building, hoping to obtain a profit by selling out when the value has appreciated. Some investors may, of course, seek not capital appreciation, but primarily a safe investment giving fairly good returns for a few years, with the intention of moving into some other sphere of investment when conditions improve. Here they will consider the present and future level of rents and, maybe, to some extent, the future value of the building.

Whether or not a particular individual with capital to invest will choose to invest in buildings will depend on his knowledge of other forms of investment, on his personal preferences, and similar factors; and one must remember that investment in property is, and has been, a favourite form of investment by all classes in society and offers a good return on capital with a minimum risk of serious capital loss. Moreover, " bricks and mortar " are the one form of investment in which the investor can actually see the concrete manifestation of his investment, and he may like, perhaps, to undertake some of the maintenance of the building—very important factors for the working, and possibly also the middle classes.

The factors involved in determining the supply for occupation by investors in residential buildings are prices of buildings, costs of repairs, rents, the long-term rate of interest (determining the annual capital cost whether the house is bought outright or with a mortgage), and expectations of future changes in these variables.

Municipal Housing Schemes.

Housing schemes of municipalities, when actually carried out, are demands for and supplies of buildings for ownership, supplies of buildings for occupation, and demands for building activity. However, since housing schemes are initiated by municipalities who take into account many non-economic factors, we cannot analyse here exactly what factors enter into the determination of this section of demand for residential buildings. We can only mention such schemes as important factors in the total supply of buildings for occupation, therefore in the demand for residential buildings for ownership, and therefore in the total demand for building activity.

(b) *Factory and Commercial Buildings*

In the case of factory and commercial buildings the vast majority of firms are in the same position as owner-occupiers of residential buildings. This means that they supply the buildings for occupation which they themselves demand. Since we have already considered the factors in the demand for factory and commercial buildings for occupation, we have therefore already considered the factors in the supply for occupation.

The investor in factory and commercial buildings (usually the firm in occupation) is exactly the same, from our point of view, as the investor in residential buildings, except for the fact that factory and commercial buildings are much more specific and there is, therefore, more probability of investment being made in a *new* factory.

4. Equilibrium Between Demand and Supply for Occupation

We have now examined the determination of the demand schedules and supply schedules of buildings for occupation, residential, factory, and commercial. These, in turn, determine the levels of rents. This is easily seen when we assume only one type of building and only one rental class in only one area, since there will finally emerge such a level of rent as will equate the supply of these buildings for occupation to the demand for occupation. When there are several types of buildings, more than one rental class, and many areas, and when buildings can be altered and repaired and thereby shifted from one rental class to another, we have to deal with a large number of supply and demand schedules, each pair of which result in one equilibrium rent. In equilibrium the whole complex of rents is determined by the fact that, in every rental class and in every area, supply for occupation equals the demand for occupation at the equilibrium rent. We must remember, of course, that every demand or supply schedule in any rental class in any area depends upon the nexus of rents in many rental classes in many areas, but this does not affect our analysis. The whole problem clearly bristles with difficulties in all directions, but through and behind them all lies the fundamental conception that, in equilibrium, the whole complex of rents is determined by the fact that in every rental class in every area, supply for occupation equals demand for occupation at the equilibrium rent. In the real world equilibrium can never be attained, but forces are ever present tending to bring about such an equilibrium. Here, beyond doubt, lies the key to the solution of most problems connected with building.

CHAPTER V

A DYNAMIC ECONOMY: ECONOMIC FACTORS (*contd.*)

BUILDINGS FOR OWNERSHIP AND BUILDING ACTIVITY

1. Buildings for Ownership: Demand

As we have seen, there is a close connection between the supply of buildings for occupation and the demand for buildings for ownership. Before an individual (owner-occupier, investor, government, or local authority) can supply a building for occupation, he must demand a building for ownership. It follows, therefore, that, as the demand for ownership arises out of the supply for occupation, the factors in the demand for buildings for ownership have already been considered in the last chapter.

2. Buildings for Ownership: Supply

When all factors in the demand for buildings for occupation and for ownership are constant, it is obvious that a change in the number of buildings in existence alters the supply schedule of buildings for ownership, *i.e.* the number of buildings offered at various prices. The simplest way of revealing the factors influencing supply for ownership is, therefore, to consider which factors change the number of buildings in existence in different rental classes in different areas.

The first and most obvious factor is the physical wearing out of buildings, or the number of buildings falling to be replaced each year. If these buildings are not replaced, the number of buildings in existence will fall. Similarly, buildings have an economic life which is, of course, elastic, and when this is ended they are either left unoccupied or demolished and rebuilt. If new buildings are erected of the same type as the old, there is no alteration in the number of buildings in existence of any type, but usually the new buildings are of that type for which demand for ownership is most intense; and we then meet the problem of deciding whether the loss of old (and obsolete) buildings and the gain of new buildings shall be regarded as an alteration in supply. In such a case the supply of buildings in one rental class has been reduced through demolitions and the supply of buildings in another rental class has been increased through new building. And consequently there will be an alteration in the supply schedules for ownership and in the equilibrium of the system. The main influence upon the numbers of houses in each rental class comes, however, not from replacements but from new building, and in the following pages we consider the main factors involved in the supply of new buildings for ownership.

(a) *Residential Buildings*

The Owner-occupier.

There is no alteration in the number of houses in existence when a would-be owner-occupier purchases an existing building, except in so far as his purchase has repercussions through the actions of the seller or through effects on the prices of buildings. But when he has a house built he makes an addition to the number of buildings in existence in some rental class, and thereby affects the supply for ownership. In this case the owner-occupier supplies the building for ownership to satisfy his own demand. At the same time, if he formerly rented a house, he affects the demand for occupation. Similar considerations obviously apply when the owner-occupier sells his house. The factors influencing his decisions have already been examined in our section on the supply for occupation.[1] Whether he buys an old house or a new house depends upon his income, his tastes, and the relative costs of buying and running old and new houses.

The Investor.

He is in exactly the same position as the owner-occupier as regards the supply of houses for ownership, except that,

[1] See pp. 62 to 64.

since he does not occupy his property, he has not the same aversion to selling. The factors involved in the supply for ownership by investors were considered under the supply for occupation.[1]

The Speculative Builder.

He concentrates entirely upon the building of houses and their supply for ownership. He accounts for a very large proportion of the total output of new residential buildings, and it is extremely important, therefore, to analyse the factors which determine the output of speculative builders.

The speculative builder may be a small firm, a large company, or a housing syndicate, and may build not only middle- and working-class houses but also warehouses along the river, offices in the city and shops in the West End. The speculative builder may build to let or to sell, but in the vast majority of cases he builds to sell, since he has only a limited amount of capital at his disposal.

The speculative builder is influenced by many factors. Technical changes may induce him to build; the modern "labour-saving" house, for instance, has given the speculative builder plenty of scope in this direction. If tastes in houses alter, the speculative builder immediately responds by producing those types which he thinks will induce investors and owner-occupiers to purchase. The geographical distribution of population within the country is always changing, and the speculative builder will always be found most active in those receiving areas where there is a shortage of accommodation. Developments of transport facilities, through their effects upon the distribution of population in urban and suburban areas, are also important factors. Finally, after a period of inactivity in building (due to such causes as a high rate of interest) the replacements, repairs, and alterations which should have followed the wastage of property will have accumulated and "building need" thereby increased. In such a situation the number of unoccupied houses[2] will be very small, prices of houses will

[1] See pp. 64 and 65.

[2] For a full discussion of unoccupied houses see H. W. Robinson, "A Note on Unoccupied Houses," *Review of Economic Studies*, June, 1939.

have risen and the speculative builder will be induced to build. Usually, however, the speculative builder does not wait for demand to show itself before building but tries to anticipate it. For this reason expectations of demand for occupation, and of the interest rate and costs of building are extremely important for him.

Another important factor is that of finance. Large-scale speculative builders raise capital mainly by the issue of share capital, and possess an advantage over the small builder in the low costs of building per house and, when the houses are let, in management of the property. The small speculative builder, however, who forms the main nucleus of the speculative builders, often depends upon overdrafts from the banks for his current expenses and on credit from builders' merchants, who in turn have credit from the raw materials producers. Overdrafts are usually guaranteed by a mortgage on the building site or on the unbuilt houses. In all these cases, therefore, the rate of interest is an important factor, but varies in importance according to the particular method of finance. Fluctuations in the rate of interest will, therefore, have widely different effects in different cases.

The speculative builder knows roughly what his interest, cost of building, and other charges are going to be, and he also knows what the prices and rentals of buildings are at the moment. He can, therefore, determine whether, if these factors remain constant during the time required to build, he can make a profit by building and selling. Most of the buildings built by the speculative builder can be erected within three to six months, so that, except in times of rapidly rising costs, there is usually not much need to consider probable changes in the relevant factors during this time. Furthermore, the speculative builder usually aims at a margin large enough to cover changes which are likely to occur in these factors. Thus we can say that the number of houses built by speculative builders is a function of the rate of interest, the level of building costs, and the selling price of houses.

Municipalities.

They supply the buildings for ownership, which they themselves demand. In this case, however, the addition to the supply of buildings usually goes hand in hand with the demolition of other buildings, owing to slum-clearance schemes, and the change in the number of buildings in existence is smaller than would be indicated by the figures of houses built by local authorities.

(b) *Factory and Commercial Buildings*

Apart from those offices and shops built by speculative builders, most factory and commercial buildings are erected by the occupiers who have them built to contract. Here again, therefore, these people supply the buildings for ownership to satisfy their own demand and the factors involved have already been considered in the previous section on the supply for occupation.[1]

3. Equilibrium Between Demand and Supply for Ownership

The interaction of the demand schedule for ownership with the supply schedule for ownership in each rental class in each area results in the price of each class of building in each area. It must be borne in mind that the supply schedule for ownership includes *unbuilt* (*i.e.*, potential) buildings, since, above a certain price, not only will existing buildings be offered but new buildings will be erected by owner-occupiers, investors, and speculative builders. At the same time, given the rate of interest and building costs, there will be a definite demand from owner-occupiers in each rental class, the remainder of the houses being owned by investors and let to rent-payers. Thus, in equilibrium, the ratio of owner-occupiers to rent-payers in each class is determined. It may happen that this equilibrium can be attained ultimately only if new buildings are erected, and in this case there will be a demand for building activity until equilibrium is attained.

We have here the same problem as that in the previous

[1] See pp. 59 to 61.

chapter on rents, namely, the problem of the determination of a whole *complex* of prices of buildings which are capable of being altered and thereby shifted into different rental classes. But here again the conception of equality of supply and demand in equilibrium enables us to see clearly how prices of different classes of buildings in different areas tend to settle down to levels which ensure that supply equals demand in every rental class in every area. The transference of buildings from one rental class to another and from one type to another will actually speed up the process of adjustment, since it usually requires less time to alter or add to a building than to build an entirely new one.

4. Building Activity: Demand

The demand for building activity first of all arises as a direct result of the demand for and supply of buildings for ownership, which in turn depend on supply and demand for occupation. The demand for buildings for ownership is satisfied either by existing buildings or by new buildings; if it is satisfied by existing buildings, no demand for building activity for new buildings arises, while if it is satisfied by new buildings (*i.e.* by the supply of new buildings for ownership), a demand for building activity for the building of the new structures is obviously created. The demand for and supply of buildings for occupation are linked up with the demand for building activity for repairs (both for maintenance and for decorations), and, in times of changing composition demand (size, type and rental class), for alterations. There are, therefore, two sections of demand for building activity: a fairly constant demand for repairs and alterations, and a demand which depends upon the extent of new building (including demolition).

We now examine whether, and how, the various persons interested in buildings demand building activity. In those instances where a demand for building activity is observed it is obviously connected with the supply of buildings for ownership or the supply of buildings for occupation; and the factors already considered under these headings are, indirectly, also the factors involved in the demand for building activity.

(a) *New Residential Buildings*

The Rent-payer and Owner-occupier.

The rent-payer has little direct influence on the demand for building activity, since he usually is not responsible for repairs. The owner-occupier, on the other hand, demands building activity for repairs, and perhaps alterations, when he occupies an existing house. He demands building activity for construction when he has a house built, and thereafter demands building activity for repairs, and maybe alterations. He has no influence upon the demand for building activity if he purchases a new house already built, except in so far as he demands building activity for repairs, and maybe alterations.

The Investor.

From the point of view of the demand for building activity the investor can be regarded as identical with the owner-occupier. The only difference in behaviour arises in the demand for building activity for repairs; the investor is interested in maximising his *money* income (rent minus running expenses), while the owner-occupier is interested in maximising his *psychic* income, and may, and usually does, spend far more on repairs and alterations.

The Speculative Builder.

The speculative builder, building houses mainly for the owner-occupier and the investor, demands building activity for new construction. He only influences the demand for building activity for repairs and alterations when he purchases an existing building and improves it by carrying out alterations, or when he actually maintains the buildings as an investment, and therefore takes on the rôle of an investor in houses. In all these cases, of course, he supplies the building activity to satisfy his own demand.

Municipalities.

Municipalities demand building activity for new construction when they initiate housing schemes, and thereafter demand building activity for repairs (and perhaps alterations) when they let the houses built under their schemes.

(b) *New Factory and Commercial Buildings*

The continued use of factory and commercial buildings involves demand for building activity for repairs. Where vacant existing buildings are adapted to new uses, there is a demand for building activity for alterations. Where *new* factories and commercial buildings are erected there is a demand for building activity for new construction, and subsequently an addition to the demand for repairs and alterations, though this will be small during the early years of the life of the new buildings.

Each firm has its own requirements with respect to lay-out of plant and workshops, and therefore a certain amount of alteration is usually required before an old factory can be used for production, a fact which is, of course, considered when deciding to have an existing factory rather than to have a new one built. In the case of shops and offices, the alterations required are not so extensive as in the case of factories containing equipment, since the alterations are then concerned mainly with office and shop fittings, including shop-fronts. The demand is, in many cases, for homogeneous units of floor-space rather than for particular design and lay-out of buildings.

As in the case of supply of buildings for occupation, the level of business activity, the proportion of vacant premises, the rate of interest, and costs of building can be regarded as main factors in the demand for building activity for factories and commercial buildings generally. But, as in all our problems, we should take account of varations from area to area when considering building activity in the country as a whole; while the number of vacancies may be large in South Wales, it may be almost zero in London. Similarly, the level of business activity and the level of building costs in the whole country take no account of regional differences.

(c) *Public Works and Miscellaneous*

In the case of public works, the local authorities and government departments are in the same position with respect to demand for building activity as municipalities above, except that the type of building activity demanded is different—namely, the services of the public works contractors. The societies and religious orders behave in the same way as the investor in houses.

(d) *Demolition, Repairs and Alterations*

It must be remembered that whenever a building is demolished there is a demand for " building activity " for this purpose, so that an important question when considering new building is whether new buildings are erected upon vacant sites or upon sites previously occupied. This will depend upon the cost of demolition and the costs and advantages of alternative sites. The execution of repairs and alterations also involves a demand for building activity. The factors involved here are those considered under " supply for occupation ", and particularly important are those involved in the supply of buildings for occupation in one rental class by the alteration and repair of buildings from another class. These factors are rents of various rental classes, costs of building, and the rate of interest. Expectations are very important, since much of the alteration and repair of buildings is done in anticipation of changes in rents.

5. Building Activity: Supply

It still remains to be considered what factors are operative on the supply schedule for building activity—*i.e.* what factors influence the builder in supplying to satisfy the demand for building activity.

On pages 8 to 10 we considered the different types of firms engaged on building work. The following was the classification used:

(*a*) Large general contractors, public works contractors and small general contractors;

(*b*) Jobbing builders; painters and decorators;
(*c*) Speculative builders; and
(*d*) Sub-contractors.

In the following analysis we shall group together (*a*) and (*d*), since they are firms supplying building activity on long-time contract. The groups (*b*) and (*c*) demand separate treatment.

Builders Working on Long Contracts.

The length of time required to complete a building varies according to its nature. A large factory or public building requires a very long time to complete, while a small house can be built within three months. Most of the factory and commercial buildings and many residential buildings are built to contract, *i.e.* the builder contracts to complete the erection within a specified time at a specified cost. Under present methods of contracting the specification and drawings may or may not be incorporated in the contract, but, as a bill of quantities is always drawn up, the precise nature of the work to be done is always fully known to both parties, and the architect ensures that the work actually carried out conforms to the specifications. Most contracts are what is known as "lump-sum contracts", that is, a contract in which a definite lump sum is agreed on by the contractor and building-owner as the cost of the building in its finished state. Finally the contract may or may not provide for a "date for completion", but the majority do have this provision, and in actual fact, when no date is fixed, the work must be performed within a reasonable time. Thus it is clear that the work to be done is perfectly well defined and therefore known with certainty, and that the cost of the finished building and the time within which the building can be built at that cost have to be forecast by the contractor.

It must not be forgotten that the contractor must usually send in a competitive tender for the contract, and he must therefore forecast the *minimum* cost, or the *shortest* time at a low cost if he is to obtain the contract. Moreover, he can sub-let parts of the contract and thereby shift the responsibility of forecasting to the sub-contractors, who are then in the same position as the contractors. Sub-letting obviously involves a greater distribution of risk.

Since the contractor is an expert we must, in this analysis, assume that, knowing the specifications, the bill of quantities, the difficulties connected with the site, transport, etc., he knows, with great exactitude, what work and what difficulties he is to encounter in completing the contract. Thus his forecasting will be confined to: (i) prices of his raw materials, plant, equipment, labour, transport, etc., (ii) ease of obtaining supplies of labour, raw materials, etc., at these prices. However, we might argue that, in all except the most abnormal situations, the supplies of labour, raw materials, and so on can be obtained if a sufficiently high price is offered for them, so that our contractor is ultimately considering the future of the prices of the labour, raw materials, etc., which are required to complete the contract. It is often the case, however, in the building industry, that a shortage of factors of production leads to difficulties in obtaining supplies at any price as well as to a rise in the prices of factors.

Since the contractor must finance the work in the interval between receiving the contract and receiving payment, he must include in his considerations the interest on his capital expenditure during construction. Thus the rate of interest and its estimated changes also influence the contractor in determining the estimate he submits, although this item in costs is of relatively small importance except in the case of large contracts which involve a long period of construction.

The costs of building will, for this type of contractor, be influenced, in the large, by these factors, and though some contractors will be unduly optimistic, some unduly pessimistic, we can conceive that, on the whole, changes in the general level of these variables will bring about corresponding changes in the contract price of buildings.

Jobbing Builders, Painters and Decorators.

In the case of that class of builders called, in our classification, " jobbing builders ", the length of time for which they have to supply building activity is short, since they are mainly concerned with repair work, decorating, and remodelling. In this case, therefore, the task of forecasting prices is much easier, and we can safely assume that the present cost of repairs, decorations, or alterations alone is relevant. Since the amount of capital laid out is small, and since many of these builders receive credit from the builders' merchants and only have to pay weekly wages bills before receiving payment, the rate of interest is not such an important factor, and can be neglected.

In this case, therefore, we can limit the factors influencing supply to the existing costs of building unless costs are fluctuating very violently.

Speculative Builders.

These builders supply building activity to satisfy their own demand for building activity and have already been considered under supply for ownership.[1] The amount of building activity supplied by them obviously depends upon the same factors as were considered in that section.

We must conclude that the supply of building activity as a whole depends upon costs of factors of production (materials, labour and equipment), the rate of interest, the selling price of buildings (a factor special to the speculative builder), and expectations regarding future changes in these variables.

6. The Factors Determining Equilibrium Building Activity

We have now examined, in detail, the influences which operate upon the supply of and demand for buildings for ownership and occupation, and for building activity. It only remains for us to consider what determines the actual amount of building activity which is carried on at any given moment. The amount of building activity which is carried on at any moment of time is determined by the interaction of the supply of and demand for building activity. We have, on the one hand, the different quantities of building

[1] See pp. 70 and 71.

activity which would be demanded at different prices per unit and, on the other hand, the different quantities of building activity which would be supplied at different prices per unit, remembering, of course, that a unit of building activity is a combination of materials, labour and equipment.[1] Equilibrium is obtained when supply is equal to demand, and this particular building activity can be called the equilibrium level of building activity. This equality also determines the level of building costs, and, if we sub-divide building activity into homogeneous parts such as bricks, cement, bricklayers' labour, and so on, we shall obtain, from the various supply and demand schedules, the level of building activity and costs for each part.

Now, we have seen that the demand for building activity depends upon the values of many demographic and economic variables, while supply depends upon the values of other economic variables. Both, moreover, depend upon the various items entering into building costs. Equilibrium building activity is, therefore, dependent upon all those factors which enter into the supply of and demand for building activity which we have considered in the preceding chapters.

We can therefore summarise our analysis by drawing up a list of the factors which predominate in the determination of the equilibrium level of building activity. It may be noted that not all of the factors are independent.

A. *Residential Building Activity*

Factors :

(1) " Building need."
(2) Spatial movements of population.
(3) National income.
(4) Cost of living (apart from rent).
(5) Rent ; (*a*) ground rent, (*b*) house rent.
(6) Rates.
(7) Costs of building activity (new buildings, demolition, repairs and alterations).

[1] At any one price the composition of the unit of building activity may vary so long as its cost remains the same.

(8) Mortgage (or building society) rate of interest.
(9) Proportion of capital mortgageable.
(10) Building society period of repayment.
(11) Proportion of unoccupied houses.
(12) Business activity.
(13) Government subsidies.
(14) Demolition policy.
(15) Tastes.
(16) Building Society advertisements.
(17) Anticipations of changes in these variables.

B. *Factory and Commercial Building Activity*

Factors :

(1) Spatial movements of industry.
(2) Business activity.
(3) The long-term rate of interest.
(4) Factors which have already been enumerated in section A—National income, costs of building activity, vacant factories and commercial buildings.
(5) Anticipated changes in all these variables.

7. The Relationship Between Rent, Price and Building Costs

We have shown that the levels of rents, prices, and building costs are each determined by the interaction of a demand schedule and a supply schedule. At the same time it is obvious that rents, prices of buildings, and building costs are intimately connected. This can be seen clearly if we consider the different demand and supply schedules.

Ignoring for the moment the numerous other factors and concentrating only on the most important variables, we have,

A. Demand for occupation depends on rent.

B. Supply for occupation depends on rent, price, building costs, and the rate of interest.

C. Demand for ownership depends on rent, price, building costs, and the rate of interest.

D. Supply for ownership depends on rent, price, building costs, and the rate of interest.

E. Demand for building activity depends upon rent, price, building costs, and the rate of interest.

F. Supply of building activity depends on building costs.

Now, as $A = B$, $C = D$ and $E = F$ in equilibrium, and as other factors, including the rate of interest, are given, we have three equations which solve the problem of determining the three unknowns, rent, price, and building costs. It is clear also that, as all three are determined simultaneously, each of these depends upon the other two. We can, however, discover the relationship between them *a priori*. Suppose, for the moment, there is one type of building in one rental class in one area. In equilibrium price must equal the cost of construction, if we include normal profit of entrepreneurs in cost, otherwise (i) if price is greater than cost it pays to construct buildings and sell in the market, (ii) if price is less than cost it pays to buy rather than build, and no new building goes on. In both cases demand for ownership and demand for building activity change, and price and cost are forced up or down until they reach equality. This statement must be modified by the fact that old buildings in any rental class are of less value than new ones (neglecting " quasi rents ") simply because of their age, and the price can then diverge from the replacement cost by an amount sufficient to compensate for the age of the structure.

Again, the price of the building must equal the sum of (*a*) the discounted net receipts (rent minus running expenses) over the length of life remaining in the building, minus an allowance for (*b*) the normal proportion of unoccupied buildings, due to movement of population between houses but not migration, and (*c*) the depreciation of the property due to wastage, population changes, spatial movement of population and industry, etc.; the rate of interest is, of course, an important factor in the discounting. Here again there can be no persistent divergence, since (i) if price is greater than this sum it pays to sell houses, so that the supply for ownership increases (through new building) while the supply for occupation falls, and the price must fall or more houses must be built and/or rent must rise,[1] and (ii) if price is less than this sum it pays to buy houses and let them, so that the demand for ownership and the supply for occupation rise, and price must rise and rent fall. In both cases the price is forced to equality with the algebraic sum of the components (*a*), (*b*), and (*c*).

When we turn to reality we see not one type of building in one rental class in one area, but several types in several rental classes in many areas. Moreover, the fact that a building can be repaired, altered, and decorated means that the number of buildings in any one class can be altered, not only by new building, but by transformation of buildings by repairs and alterations in other rental classes. Our problem is, therefore, more complex.

But if we examine the problem carefully, we see that our argument is unaffected if we consider only one single class of building in one area at a time, and consider its rent and its price as that rent and that price which can be obtained if the building is kept in that rental class. In that case, our observations above still hold true. Furthermore, since it is easier to transform (within a certain limited range) a building from one rental class to another than to construct a new building, it follows that the supply of buildings for ownership (and therefore for occupation) in any one rental class is elastic, and that the forces tending towards equilibrium are intensified, and equilibrium therefore achieved more rapidly. Thus, if the price of a building in a particular class rises above the equilibrium level, not only are new houses built, but houses in other rental classes are transformed and brought into this rental class, until, in equilibrium, the equalities hold good. On the other hand, since it is impossible to move buildings from one area to another, this elasticity of supply is limited to the movement of buildings between rental classes in one area only.

[1] Rent restrictions may, however, transfer the task of re-adjustment to prices of buildings.

8. How the Quantity of Building Activity is Determined

To summarise our consideration of a dynamic economy let us now examine what factors determine the tempo of building activity at any moment of time. We shall find that the system of analysis developed above provides us with a ready means of solving this problem.

The first step towards a solution is to satisfy ourselves concerning what are the given data, necessary and sufficient to determine the amount of building activity expended at each point of time. Confining attention to residential building (*i.e.* assuming only residential buildings to be required), the following factors are sufficient:

(*a*) The number of families;

(*b*) The tastes of the families;

(*c*) The incomes of the families and prices of all commodities.

The above determine the demand schedules for occupation in all rental classes.

(*d*) Building costs at various levels of output which are dependent upon the natural resources and the technical conditions of production;

(*e*) The number of family accommodations of each rental class already in existence, and the supply schedules relating the number of these family accommodations which would be offered for occupation to various levels of rent;

(*f*) The amounts of annual repairs required to maintain family accommodations in their respective rental classes;

(*g*) The amounts of building activity required to shift (by alteration) each house from its own rental class into each of the others and

(*h*) The rate of interest and the length-of-life indifference curves; these also determine the length of life of buildings.[1]

[1] See Note to Chapter II.

Our next step is to simplify the problem by supposing that all families are exactly alike and that all houses are of one type and one rental class. We also assume that the owner-occupier is exactly similar in his behaviour to the rent-payer, that the population is rigidly separated into owners and occupiers (the owner-occupier being both owner and occupier is merely incidental), and that there are no rates. Our problem then becomes one of explaining how the factors above operate in determining the supply and demand schedules in the three markets: (i) buildings for occupation, (ii) buildings for ownership, and (iii) building activity. Finally we have to explain how equilibrium is attained in the three markets simultaneously.

Incomes and tastes of the families and prices of all commodities determine the demand curve of buildings for occupation *AB* (see Figure 2), which relates rent with the number of family accommodation which would be demanded at that rent. This curve implies, of course, that the number of families per accommodation (number of families ÷ number of accommodations) is also related to the level of rent.

This demand schedule, in conjunction with the given rate of interest and the supply schedule for occupation, also determines the demand curve of *new* buildings for ownership *CD*, which relates the price of new buildings with the number which would be demanded at that price. At any price of the building there will be a certain rental, determined by the rate of interest and the length of life of the building, at which it just pays the building-owner to let. We know the number of houses which can be let at this rent (from the demand curve of buildings for occupation *AB*), and hence the number of new family accommodations which are demanded for ownership at this price, will be the number of family accommodations demanded at this rental *minus* the number of existing family accommodations offered at this rental (determined from the given supply curve of existing buildings for occupation *KL*). We obtain, therefore, by considering the whole range of prices of buildings, a complete demand curve of new buildings for ownership, *CD*.

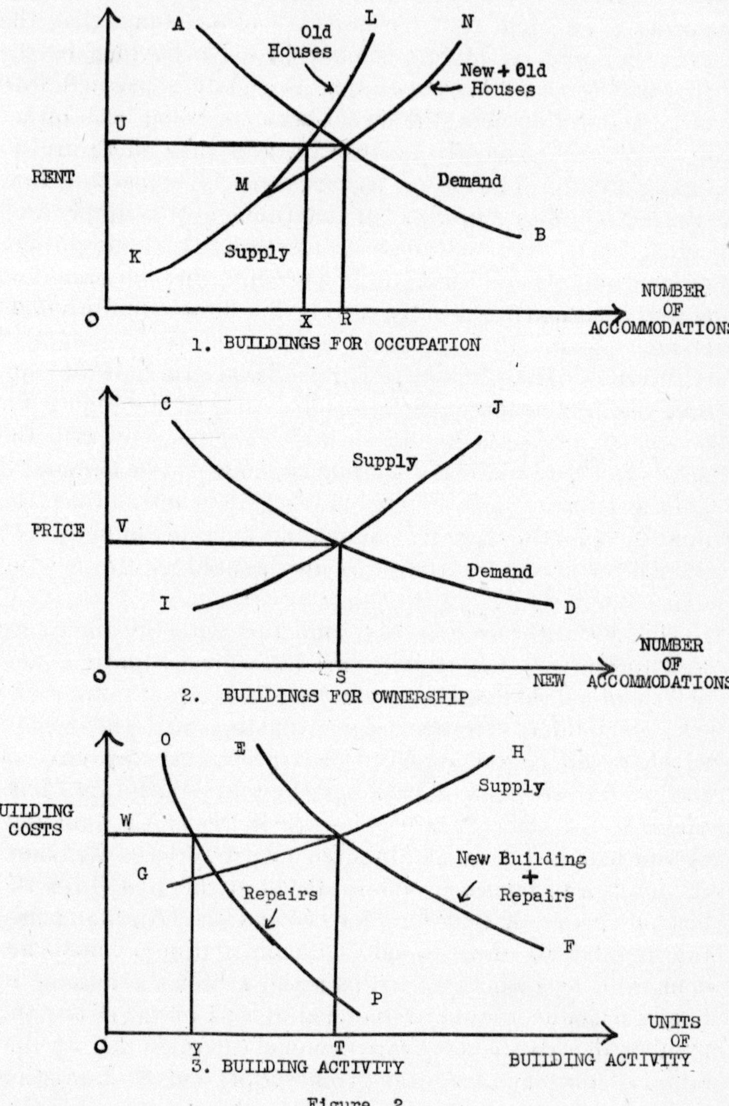
A
L
N
Old Houses
New + Old Houses
U
RENT
M
Demand
B
K
Supply
O
X
R
NUMBER OF ACCOMMODATIONS
1. BUILDINGS FOR OCCUPATION
C
J
Supply
PRICE
V
Demand
I
D
O
S
NUMBER OF NEW ACCOMMODATIONS
2. BUILDINGS FOR OWNERSHIP
O
E
H
Supply
BUILDING COSTS
W
G
New Building + Repairs
Repairs
F
P
O
Y
T
UNITS OF BUILDING ACTIVITY
3. BUILDING ACTIVITY

Figure 2

Replacement of old houses is the same as the provision of *new* houses (except for the cost of demolition), and we shall consider them identical from now on.

The demand schedule of new buildings for ownership helps to determine the demand for building activity. Since the price of the building must equal the cost of building, and since each new accommodation requires a certain number of units of building activity, we can derive a demand curve of building activity from the demand schedule for new buildings for ownership simply by transforming the "price" axis into a "building costs" axis and the "number of new accommodations" axis into a "units of building activity" axis. The aggregate demand curve of building activity will, however, be dependent also upon the demand curve of building activity for repairs to existing buildings OP—which relates the building activity demanded for repairs with building costs, and therefore with the level of rents.

The complete demand curve of building activity EF is found by summing the two curves—one of new buildings for ownership and one of repairs to existing buildings.

The supply curve of building activity GH is part of the given data. It also determines the supply curve of new buildings for ownership IJ, because price must equal the cost of building and because there is a certain number of units of building activity required to construct a building. In other words, the supply curve of building activity is readily transformable into the supply curve of new buildings for ownership. The latter curve is readily transformable, in turn, into the supply curve of new buildings for occupation; the rate of interest and the length of life of the buildings set a relation between the price of the building and the rent at which it can be let, so that the supply of new houses at any price implies the supply of these buildings at a certain rental. Hence the supply curve of new buildings for ownership immediately gives the supply curve of new houses for occupation. When we add this supply curve of *new* houses for occupation to the supply curve of *existing* houses for occupation, we obtain the complete supply curve of buildings for occupation MN.

We now have six curves, and equilibrium is found in each market at the intersection of the supply curve with the demand curve. The points of intersection determine rent OU (from demand and supply for occupation), price of buildings OV (from demand and supply for ownership), and building costs OW (from demand and supply of building activity). Owing to the method of construction of the curves, they show the correct relationship between rent, price, and building costs—costs equal price, and discounted rents over the life of the building equal costs and price. There is also the correct relationship between building activity and the number of new accommodations built. The number of houses which are built OS (which equals XR) is determined by the equilibrium between supply and demand for building activity, which tells us how many units of building activity will be expended on repairs ($= OY$), on new accommodations ($= YT$), and at what cost. We know therefore how many new houses will be built for ownership, their price, and the rental at which they will be let, and also the number of old houses ($= OX$) which are let at the equilibrium rent.

It may be objected that our curves sometimes refer to time present, as when we consider the supply curve of existing houses for occupation, and sometimes to time future, as in the case of the supply curve of new houses for occupation. But if we remember that these curves tell us how many houses would ultimately be offered for occupation at any level of rent, how many new houses would ultimately be demanded for ownership at any price, and so on, then it becomes clear that the equilibrium described by these curves is the *ultimate* equilibrium of the system *for the unit of time considered ;* if the data and expectations remain constant, and tells us how much building activity is expended during this period of time. We have always assumed, in supply schedules of building activity, that the quantity of building activity was to be related to an arbitrary unit of time—it is only by so doing that the supply schedule can have any meaning; it then gives the costs of various *rates* at which building activity could be expended. As time goes on all the given data are continually changing and a new equilibrium is required in the next unit of time. Since time can be divided into units as small as we please, we can, by making the unit period of time small enough, describe the course of building activity as a succession of attempts to get into the position of equilibrium dictated by the data at each point of time—in other words, we can describe a continuous course of building activity.

When we introduce a whole complex of rental classes, the problem becomes much more complicated, since houses in any rental class can be repaired and altered, and thereby shifted into other rental classes. The amount of building activity required to effect this transformation will of course depend upon the rental classes from which and into which the house is moved. The problem is, however, very much simplified if we consider as many supply and demand schedules, both for occupation and ownership, as there are rental classes, and if we are careful to include alterable houses in the supply schedules and the building activity required for alterations in the demand schedule for building activity. We shall then, in an exactly similar manner to that above, obtain all the curves necessary to determine (*a*) rents in all rental classes, (*b*) prices of buildings in all rental classes, and (*c*) the rate at which building activity is expended at any moment of time on (i) the building of new houses, (ii) alterations to existing buildings, and (iii) repairs.

It is easy to see, from this analysis, how changes in the rate of interest or building costs affect the equilibrium. If the rate of interest falls, for example, the supply curve of occupation *MN*, the demand curve of ownership *CD*, and the demand curve of building activity *EF* are shifted to the right (since the relationship between rent and price has been altered). Hence more houses will be built, more will be let, price will be higher, and rental will be lower. If building costs fall, the supply curve of building activity *GH*, the supply curve of buildings for ownership *IJ*, and the supply curve of buildings for occupation *GH* are shifted to the right and the result is more new building, lower rents, lower prices, and more houses let.

The amount of building activity required for factory and

commercial building depends upon the following necessary and sufficient factors, if we assume no residential building:

(*a*) The tastes and incomes of the population (which determine the demand schedules for all commodities and services);

(*b*) The cost curves for all commodities and services (excluding the cost curve for building activity);

These determine the demand schedule for occupation.

(*c*) The number and nature of existing factory and commercial buildings;

(*d*) The supply schedule of building activity;

(*e*) The amounts of repairs required to maintain factory and commercial buildings in their present condition;

(*f*) The amounts of building activity required to alter factory and commercial buildings in order to change the commodity or service which can be produced; and

(*g*) The rate of interest, the length-of-life indifference curves, and the length of life of the buildings.

Applying the same technique as that used in the case of residential buildings, we can determine the supply and demand schedules for occupation and ownership (usually each occupier is also the owner), and for building activity, and hence determine the equilibrium rent, price, and level of building costs. Finally, the number of new buildings, the number of alterations and repairs, and the amount of building activity expended can be determined for each point of time.

Combining the residential with the factory and commercial building activity—that is, assuming both residential and commercial building to be carried on—we merely have to form composite supply-and-demand schedules for building activity by combining the four schedules already considered. Thus the equilibrium level of building costs, the amount of building activity devoted to residential building, alterations to residential buildings, and repairs to residential buildings, the amount of building activity devoted to factory and commercial building and repairs and alterations to factory and commercial buildings, and finally the total building activity for all purposes, can be determined for each point of time.

The above analysis is not applicable merely to buildings and building activity. It applies equally well to any commodity. Since buildings are durable goods, the analysis applies strictly to durable consumers' goods and producers' goods alone. But if we reduce the length of life of the commodity, the validity of the analysis is unimpaired; it merely means that the rate of interest drops out of the analysis and that "ownership" and "occupation" are identical (for other commodities "occupation" means use), and rent and price are equal. Instead of the number of existing houses we have the stocks of the commodity, and instead of building activity we have production of the commodity. Hence the analysis is a general one of the interrelation between the three markets of productive activity, of the commodity for ownership, and the commodity for use.

It would be absurd to suggest that equilibrium is ever achieved in the real world. The adjustments in supply and demand are made far too slowly ever to keep pace with changes in the demographic and economic factors we have considered.

Furthermore, we must remember that we have abstracted from many psychological and sociological factors during this analysis, and that these might affect the validity of our results.

The following extract from a book on psychology by Dimnet illustrates how important such factors are in the real world:—

"The same gentleman . . . may come to the unexpected conclusion: I will buy that house in Surrey! Incredible! Not at all. The succession of telescoping images might be seen perfectly clearly:

"(*a*) House in Cornwall + few trains + two changes + wet winters + Joneses near = not wanted.

"(*b*) House near Godalming (recommended by agent) + good trains = near + no noisy high roads = sleep. Sleep + nearness + pine trees + sandy soil = attractive = smile = buy."

Nevertheless we can safely assume, first, that our analysis will apply when we consider large groups of persons, because these other factors will tend to cancel out; and, secondly, that while equilibrium is never attained, there are always strong economic forces tending to bring it about. We need only realise this fact to see that we can go a long way towards explaining actual economic developments in the building industry by applying the technique of our theoretical analysis. We pass on, therefore, to test our theory by using statistics of actual events in the building industry, and to determine the relative importance of the various factors in the determination of the tempo of building activity.

CHAPTER VI

THE AVAILABLE DATA

1. Limitations of the Available Data

The available data concerning building activity and the factors influencing it are found in official statistics and, occasionally, in records of private institutions such as trade unions. This means, from the very outset, that we are at a serious disadvantage, since the purposes for which the data were collected are not always those for which we are now using them. Consequently the definitions of the measurements made are not always the definitions we have given in the theoretical analysis. Moreover, definitions change in the course of time to suit official needs and to improve the collection of statistics. Hence the series are not always comparable at different times. The areas covered by the statistics also vary for different series and from time to time, once more introducing difficulties of comparability. There are also gaps in the data owing to the fact that no person has been interested in measuring some of the variables (*e.g.* the level of rents from 1850 to 1913).

Finally, there is a fundamental disadvantage which cannot possibly be corrected. All our statistics, apart from one or two minor exceptions, are obtainable only for large areas like England and Wales, Great Britain or the United Kingdom. This means that it is impossible to take account of those spatial differences within areas which were stressed so much in our theoretical analysis and which we found to be of so much importance. Our approach is, therefore, " macro-economic ". Ideally, of course, our statistics should refer to small areas, each one of which could be studied separately.[1]

However, in spite of the defects of the available data it

[1] For an analysis of post-war building activity in smaller areas than England and Wales see Dr. M. E. A. Bowley's articles in the *Review of Economic Studies*, Vol. IV, No. 3, and Vol. V, No. 3.

is possible with the various statistical methods at our disposal to draw some important conclusions. We must bear in mind, however, what each series actually means and what are its limitations. For this reason, we set out below a critical description of the available data, first, for the period 1850–1913 and, secondly, for the period 1924–37.

2. The Census of Population

Material concerning demographic factors and housing is found in the decennial Census of Population. Over the period considered (1801–1931) the material includes number of families, size of families, age and sex distribution, marital condition of the population, the number of family accommodations in existence, and the number of unoccupied houses. This information is given for England and Wales and in many cases for areas within the national area. However, in our case we shall limit our analysis to national variations in number of families, number of houses, etc., and, therefore, we always take national figures only. The definition of the various terms used, "families", "houses", "family accommodations", and so on, vary from time to time and create problems of comparability. These problems are, however, discussed later when the Census material is actually used.

3. The Data 1850–1913

(1) *Building Activity.*—The only figures existing for an index of building activity are those for employment rates in some trades engaged in the industry and statistics of inhabited houses.

(*a*) Employment statistics are derived from the unemployed percentage for the Amalgamated Society of Carpenters and Joiners only. These figures are misleading in so far as carpenters and joiners are only one section of the building trades. It does not follow that variations in employment in these two trades give an accurate indication of variations in employment in the building industry as a whole. However, we must accept these figures as the only available indication of fluctuations in employment in the building industry. They cover the period 1860–1913, and the sources are the second *Fiscal Blue Book* and the *Seventeenth Abstract of Labour Statistics*.

(*b*) The annual increase in the number of " houses " can be obtained from the Inhabited House Duty statistics in the *Annual Reports of the Commissioners of Inland Revenue* for the period 1871–1913 by adding the figures for " Houses of £20 annual value and over " and " Houses under £20 in annual value ". These figures suffer from the fact that the definition of a " house " may have changed over this period and that the size and style of houses altered considerably, thus affecting comparability. Moreover, the figures represent the total number of houses of all kinds in all parts of Great Britain, and therefore hide the changing composition (by type) of the houses built, and variations in the rate of building in different areas. Furthermore, these figures represent the difference between the number of houses built in the year and the number of houses falling to be replaced in that year, and are thus an imperfect indication of new building.

(2) *Business Activity.*—No attempt has yet been made to compile an index of business activity for pre-war years; we are compelled therefore to consider what series will give a simple but fairly accurate indication of business activity. Probably the best index is a total employment percentage (it agrees very well with the *Economist* index of business activity in post-war years); and we are fortunate in having for that purpose the Trade Union unemployment percentages for all Unions [1] from 1860 to 1913. Another index is the one of wholesale prices based from 1871 to 1913 on the old Board of Trade index number. Finally we have " Companies registered during the Year, Nominal Capital per head ", which is calculated by dividing estimated population into total capital of companies registered and is obtained

[1] These are " specially supplied by the Ministry of Labour and are corrected by the method used in *British and Foreign Trade and Industry* (the source of some of the earlier figures) ", Sir W. H. Beveridge, *Unemployment, a Problem of Industry*, p. 432.

from the *Statistical Abstracts* for the period 1863–1913. This is probably a good indication of variations in capital per head invested in new factory and commercial buildings.

These indices, together, are likely to give a fair index of the level of business activity.

(3) *National Income.*—There are only a few estimates, at scattered dates, of national income before 1913. But it seems likely that if we took the average annual number of wage-earners employed and multiplied it by the level of average annual earnings, hence obtaining the wages bill, and then added the income passing under the review of the Inland Revenue Department, we should account for a considerable part of the National Income. By multiplying an index of employment by an index of wages we have an index of variations in the "wages" section of national income, and, by taking the figures for income passing under review, we have an index of the "income" section. The employment index is the same as that used for business activity, the wages index is taken from the *Nineteenth Abstract of Labour Statistics* up to 1914, and the income passing under review is taken from the *Statistical Abstracts of the United Kingdom.* The wages index covers the period 1874–1913 and the income figures are given from 1868 to 1913. As an indication of the accuracy of the "wages" index, Professor Bowley's figures for earnings of all wage-earners in the United Kingdom (based on the *XVIIth Abstract of Labour Statistics*) are given for the period 1880–1913.

(4) *The Rate of Interest.*—Since buildings are durable commodities, it is ideally the long-term rate of interest which is required. However, an indicator of changes in rates of interest in general over this period is the Bank Rate (annual average); it is obtained from the *Statistical Abstract* and the *Board of Trade Journal.*[1]

(5) *The Cost of Living.*—No cost-of-living index number exists for this period (the Ministry of Labour index starts at 1910). But the level of wholesale prices, see (2), can be used as a very rough index.

[1] The reader is referred to p. 136 for justification of this index of rates of interest.

(6) *Building Costs.*—G. T. Jones in *Increasing Return* has calculated an index of the cost of materials in the London Building Industry from 1851 to 1922, based upon Laxton's prices given in *The Builders' Price Book* relating to materials for all trades in the building industry. The index number is formed by using constant weights in the ratio of the proportions of different materials used in the construction of an imaginary building, the proportions being based upon observations of the actual relative expenditure on brick-work, joinery, masonry, slating and tiling, plumbing, decorating and plastering about 1910. There are two major criticisms to be made concerning this index. First, the whole series of prices in Laxton show remarkable stability over quite long periods—*e.g.* the selling price of masonry remains at 90·6% of the 1910 price for 30 years! There must be something wrong here. Prices are not usually so stable that they remain *exactly* at one figure for 30 years. Moreover, variations in trade discounts were neglected. Secondly, the application of constant weights takes no account of changes in the proportions of materials used in buildings over the period. These are serious objections, but we can at least present the index for what it is worth. In a different class altogether is Professor Bowley's index of average summer weekly wages in the London building trades, which can be used to measure labour costs from 1845 to 1910.

(7) *Selling Price of Buildings.*—An index of the selling price of buildings over the period 1851–1913 can be obtained from G. T. Jones' *Increasing Return,* once more based on Laxton's *The Builders' Price Book* and on actual proportions of expenditure on various trades, and once more subject to the same criticisms as the building costs index.

(8) *Rent.*—Unfortunately there are no continuous statistics of rents since 1850. An indication of the course of rents from 1880 to 1900 can be obtained, however, from *Statistical Tables relating to Trade and Industry,* Cd. 2337, p. 31, but the figures include rates. Another index of house-rent alone has been prepared by Dr. H. W. Singer [1]

[1] In an unpublished doctoral dissertation. For a summary of the method used see Mr. Colin Clark's *National Income and National Outlay,* p. 98.

from Schedule A of income tax; unfortunately these figures can be calculated only in re-assessment years. He allows for demolitions, values of sites newly built on, and changes in the costs of building, and obtains an estimate of pure site rent which, when subtracted from rateable value, gives an estimate of house-rent. There are several drawbacks to this index, and, as it is based on G. T. Jones' index of building costs, it is subject to the same criticisms which were made on p. 97. The index is given here to show the long-period movement in the level of rent.

(9) *Building Societies.*—The figures relating to building societies are given for as far back as figures are available (*i.e.* 1891–1913) from the *Reports of the Chief Registrar of Friendly Societies* for Great Britain. From these we can obtain figures for (*a*) the number of members (*i.e.* borrowers and lenders), and (*b*) the amount advanced on mortgage during the year.

(10) "*Building Need.*"—This can be estimated for each Census year by the method given in Chapter VII; the results obtained subsequently in Table V are used.

(11) *The number of marriages* per annum can be obtained from the Annual Reports of the Registrar-General for England and Wales.

(12) *The percentage of unoccupied houses* in Census years can be obtained from the Census tables.

All these statistics are given in Appendix I and graphs of the most important series are given in Chart 4.

4. The Data 1924–37

The statistical data for the period 1924–37 is far more complete and accurate, and permit an exact analysis of the problem of the variations in building activity with the aid of mathematical statistics. A brief description of the series used is given below.

(1) *Building Activity.*—(*a*) The *Economist* has published an index of business activity which covers the period 1924–37, and one component of the complete index is an index of building activity. The latter is based on the value

of building plans approved by 146 Local Authorities in Great Britain, adjusted by an index of building costs; it is, therefore, an index measured in physical units. (*b*) Figures are available in the *Ministry of Labour Gazette* showing the percentage of insured workpeople unemployed in Great Britain and Northern Ireland in "Building" and "Public Works Contracting". (*c*) Returns of the estimated cost of buildings for which plans are approved are supplied monthly by 146 Local Authorities (population 17,810,000) covering Great Britain, but unfortunately excluding the London County Council Area. The figures are published monthly in the *Ministry of Labour Gazette* and are divided into "Dwelling-houses", "Factories and Workshops", "Shops, Offices, Warehouses, and other Business Premises", "Churches, Schools and Public Buildings", and "Other Buildings and Additions and Alterations to Existing Buildings". These figures are a good sample of the total building plans approved in Great Britain, and movements in them can be regarded as accurate indications of movements over the area as a whole. They suffer from the fact that they indicate only prospective building and there is, at present, no indication of how many of these plans are executed. Dr. Rhodes estimated that, for dwelling-houses, the actual completion of building follows the passing of the plans by about 6 months. (*d*) *The Ministry of Health* supplies figures for England and Wales of houses of annual rateable value not exceeding £78 (£105 in Greater London) provided by Local Authorities and by private enterprise (both subdivided into "assisted" and "unassisted") during the year ending 31st March.

These four series combined give a good indication of building activity and its allocation to residential building, factory and commercial building and public works.

(2) *Business Activity.*—The *Economist* index number of business activity is used. This index is formed by taking a weighted average of indices for different industries. The following is a list of the series used and the weights applied: Total Employment (10), Consumption of Coal (4), Industrial Consumption of Electricity (2), Merchandise on Railways

(4), Commercial Motor Vehicles in Use (2), Postal Receipts (3), Building Activity (2), Consumption of Iron and Steel (2), Consumption of Cotton (1), Imports of Raw Materials (2), Exports of British Manufactures (3), Shipping Movements (2), Metropolitan, Country, and Provincial Bank Clearings (4), Town Clearings (1); total weights = 42.

(3) *National Income.*—We are fortunate in having, from 1924, statistics of the whole national income for each year. These have been compiled by Mr. Colin Clark and published in his book *National Income and National Outlay.* His estimates are obtained by calculating the following elements which form the whole national income:

(i) Income which is, or might be, assessed to income tax;
(ii) Earnings of wage-earners;
(iii) Net income of agriculture;
(iv) Earnings of salary-earners and entrepreneurs with incomes below the earned-income exemption limit;
(v) Income from property held by persons not included in the income-tax assessments;
(vi) Government income from trading services and international transactions;
(vii) Payments of indirect taxation and local rates;
(viii) Expenditure on maintenance and depreciation.

For our purpose the whole national income, the sum of all these elements, is required.

We have taken Mr. Clark's figures (on p. 94) for "Home produced income", "Income from Overseas", and "Net Government Income", and since we are interested in repairs and alterations as well as new building, we have added his figures for "Maintenance and Depreciation". He omits the 1935 figure for the latter, but we have taken the same amount as was spent in 1934 and used it for 1935.

(4) *The Rate of Interest.*[1]—The following rates are ob-

[1] For a full analysis of the difficulties involved in choosing a rate of interest see p. 136.

tainable : (*a*) Bank rate, (*b*) yield on fixed interest securities, (*c*) three months rate, (*d*) average rate on building society advances, and (*e*) average building society rate to new borrowers.

(5) *Cost of Living.*—The Ministry of Labour cost-of-living index number is published in the *Ministry of Labour Gazette*, and is composed of the following elements with the following weights : Food (7½), Rent (2), Clothing (1½), Fuel and Light (1), and " Other Items ", which includes fares (½); total weights = 12½. In spite of its defects, this index can be used here to indicate changes in the cost of living. But for our purpose we require separate indices for (*a*) rent and (*b*) the cost of living apart from rent. We have therefore calculated (*b*) with the aid of the weighting system given above.

(6) *Building Costs.*—The *Economist* publishes an index of building costs which is a combination of : (i) an index of wage rates, based on a simple average of rates in London and Manchester, which include those of masons, bricklayers, carpenters and joiners, plasterers, slaters, plumbers, painters, and labourers and (ii) an index of costs of materials based on a simple average of London quotations for stone, brick, wood, tiles, joists and girders, lead, paint, and glass. The combined index is found by taking an average of the first two indices, these weights being chosen because " costs of materials " represented about one-half the value of the gross output of the building and contracting industry in 1924 and 1930. The figures concerning costs of materials and labour are for December in each year only, and have been generously supplied privately by the *Economist.*

(7) *Rent.*—The Ministry of Labour index of rent is compiled by using statistics of *controlled* rents of working-class houses from thirty-nine large towns and *decontrolled* rents from twenty-nine large towns. Until 1928 the proportion of decontrolled rents was not large enough to affect the average figure, and statistics were based on controlled rents only. Since then the figures have been adjusted by taking into account the level of decontrolled rents and the proportion of decontrolled rents in the total.

UNIVERSITY COLLEGE LIBRARY NOTTINGHAM

The information relates to rent inclusive of rates and water charges.[1]

(8) *Building Societies.*—Information can be obtained from the same source as above, and from the *Building Societies Year Book.* Series are given showing: (i) Advances on Mortgage during the year and (ii) Annual increases in Share Capital and Deposits.

(9) *Building Need.*—This can be calculated by the method given in Chapter III and the figures subsequently calculated in Table IX are reproduced here.

(10) *Marriages.*—The number of marriages per annum is obtained from the same source as for the period 1850–1913.

(11) *Wholesale Prices.*—The Board of Trade index number of wholesale prices is used. When the index was first compiled the number of quotations of representative wholesale prices included was 179, but this increased gradually to 194 in 1930; since 1930, 258 quotations (for 200 commodities) have been used. The weights are based on the 1924 Census of Production from 1924 and on the 1930 Census of Production since 1930. A geometric mean is employed.

(12) *New Capital Issues.*—These are given for the United Kingdom in the *London and Cambridge Economic Service,* and give some indication of variations in the amount of investment in factory and commercial buildings.

[1] For some persons—*e.g.* the owner-occupier—it is rent plus rates which is the important factor in determining the volume of building, but for other persons—*e.g.* the investor—it is house-rent alone which is important. In the latter case we should require to correct the Ministry's index for the level of rates. The actual course of rates in the pound in County Boroughs in England and Wales has been as follows:

1924 = 100.

1924	100·0	1930	95·0
1925	96·5	1931	94·0
1926	97·5	1932	93·5
1927	103·0	1933	94·0
1928	105·0	1934	93·5
1929	102·5	1935	93·5

The general trend in rates has been downwards, while the trend of rent plus rates has been upwards. It follows, therefore, that the trend of house-rent alone has been in the same direction as the Ministry's index.

It has also been pointed out by Mr. Frank Pick before the Royal Commission on the Geographical Distribution of the Industrial Population on 2nd March, 1938, that for London the rent plus travelling expenses of the worker was approximately constant as the worker moved outwards from the City.

No statistics exist for the number of unoccupied houses since 1924. This is unfortunate, since we should expect, from our theoretical analysis, that the number of unoccupied houses would be an important factor in determining the tempo of residential building activity.

Statistics for the period 1924–37 are given in Appendix 2 and graphs of the most important series are given in Chart 6.

CHAPTER VII

STATISTICAL ANALYSIS. DEMOGRAPHIC FACTORS

1. Introduction

The data which were described in the previous chapter, though not so detailed and accurate as we should desire them to be, permit us to make some analysis of the factors which influence building activity.

The Census material enables us to make some simple analysis of the influences of demographic factors from 1801 to 1931, to apply the analysis of "building need" to the period 1921–37, and, tentatively, to the future. The economic data for the first period, 1850 to 1913, are adequate for a broad graphical analysis. In this case a policy is adopted of smoothing out trends where they exist (wholesale prices, income, marriages) by means of an 11 year moving average. This amounts to assuming that there exists a regular cycle of 11 years and though this may not be justified, we may claim that the error involved in taking such an average is small enough to neglect when compared with the actual fluctuations of the series from the trend. A trend also exists in "wages × employment" but has not been eliminated since the superimposed fluctuations are easily distinguishable.

In the second period, that from 1924 to 1936, the period is so short that we can neglect the trend in most of the relevant series; indeed, the trend itself becomes a subject for study. The data in this period are sufficiently complete and reliable to admit of some application of the methods of mathematical statistics.

2. Statistical Analysis, 1801–1901

We commence our statistical analysis by examining the variations in demographic factors and relating them with variations in residential building.

We have indicated what are the theoretical effects of population changes on the course of residential building. What are those effects in reality? The Census of Population provides us with a wealth of material relating to population changes during the nineteenth century so that we can now examine what have been the developments in the size of the population, size of family, and age and sex distribution in England and Wales during this time, and how they have affected the amount of residential building. The relevant statistics are given in Table IV and shown graphically on Chart 1.

Table IV

Population Changes and Residential Building, 1801–1901.

(England and Wales.)

Source : The Census of Population.

Year.	Total Population.	Total No. of Families.	Increase in No. of Families.	Increase in No. of Houses.	Families per House.	Unoccupied Houses.	Persons per Family.
	(000)	(000)	%	%		%	
1801	8,893	1,897	—	—	1·203	3·65	4·69
1811	10,164	2,142	13·0	13·8	1·198	2·84	4·74
1821	12,000	2,493	16·4	16·2	1·198	3·34	4·81
1831	13,897	2,912	16·8	18·8	1·173	4·83	4·77
1841	15,914	3,312 [1]	13·7 [1]	18·6	1·125 [1]	5·88	4·80 [1]
1851	17,928	3,712	12·1 [1]	11·6	1·132	4·68	4·83
1861	20,066	4,492	21·0	14·0	1·201	4·94	4·47
1871	22,712	5,049	12·4	13·9	1·185	6·14	4·50
1881	25,974	5,633	11·6	13·4	1·166	8·00	4·61
1891	29,003	6,131	8·8	12·8	1·125	6·83	4·73
1901	32,528	7,036	14·8	14·9	1·124	7·17	4·62

[1] The number of families was incorrectly enumerated in 1841 and these figures are obtained by simple interpolation.

In Table IV and Chart 1 we consider (i) the increase in the number of families,[1] (ii) the increase in the

[1] The subjective definitions of p. 19 must now be relinquished and statistical ones chosen. Since we are dependent upon published statistics (*e.g.* the Census of Population), we must use whatever definition happens to have been chosen for collection of the data but, at the same time, we must exercise caution in interpreting the results.

Although only standardised from 1851, the definition of a "house" used in the Census of Population from 1801 to 1911 may be taken to be,

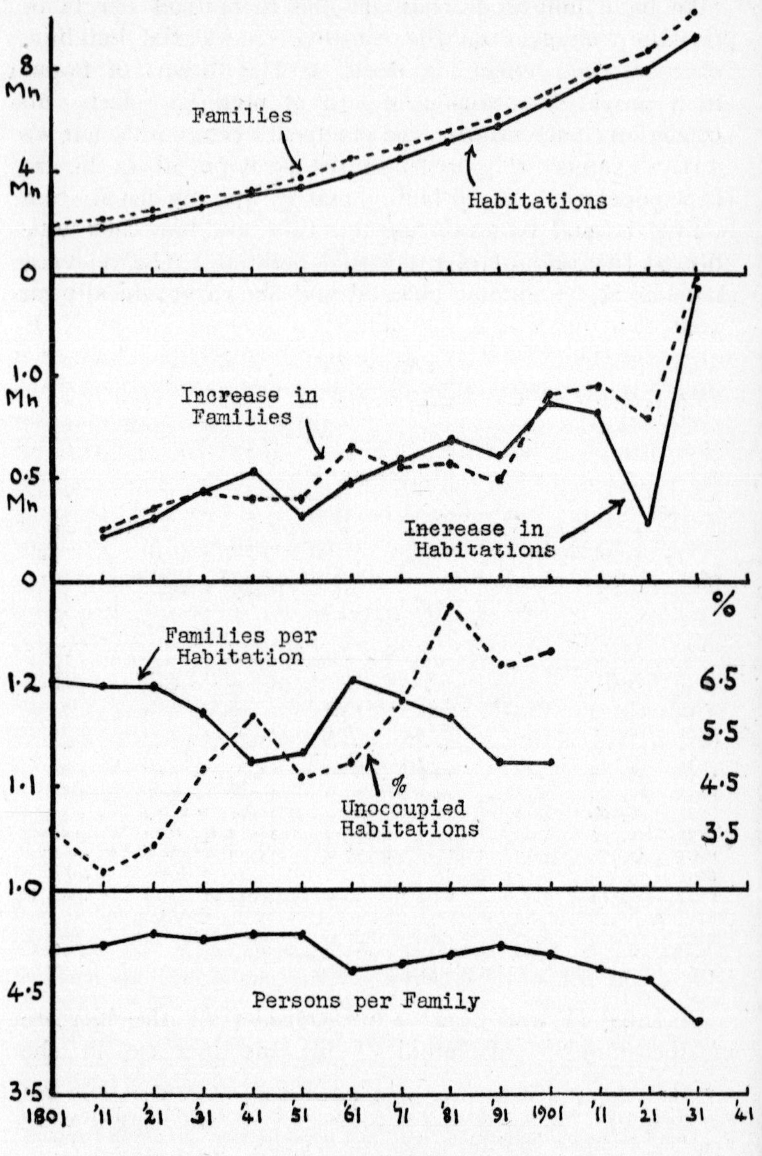

CHART 1.

Demographic Factors and Residential Building, 1801–1931.

number of houses, (iii) the number of families per house, (iv) the average size of the family, and (v) the percentage of unoccupied houses (" houses " and " families " as defined in the Census of Population). It is seen that there is a connection such as we should expect from our theoretical analysis. Over this period 1801–1901 the absolute increase in houses and the absolute increase in families are very closely correlated. Moreover in Chart 1 the two series almost overlap; on the whole there is a tendency for an increase in the number of families to be accompanied by an equivalent increase in the number of houses. There is also an indication that the percentage of unoccupied houses is inversely correlated with the number of families per dwelling. These facts are in agreement with the results of our theoretical analysis. In the long period the determining factor of changes in the number of houses built are changes in the number of families and there is a long run tendency towards the provision of one dwelling per family.[1] Furthermore, if the number of families increases relatively to the number of houses and so increases the pressure on accommodation (indicated by families per dwelling), the percentage of unoccupied houses obviously falls and vice versa. On the whole the size of the family was fairly stable over the whole period, fluctuating between 4·4 and 4·9 persons per family. There is, however, no indication that changes in the size of

" all the space within the external and party walls of a building ". It is impossible, therefore, to say which " houses " are ordinary dwelling-houses, and which are houses converted for the occupation of two or more families, maisonettes or double houses, blocks or suites of rooms inhabited by separate occupiers or even hotels, clubs and boarding-houses. In 1911, however, separate figures were given for ordinary dwelling-houses and flats, and finally, since 1921, a new unit of accommodation, the " structurally separate dwelling " (defined on p. 19) has been used.

On the other hand the definition of a " private family " has remained unchanged since 1801. A private family consists of any person or persons owning the house, or paying rent, whether (as a tenant) for the whole of the house, or (as a lodger) for any distinct floor or apartment. Lodgers at a common table who pay for their subsistence and lodging are, however, not regarded as separate families. The enumerated number of families is, therefore, always less than the number of families as defined on p. 19 in so far as there are any persons at a common table who would, if it were possible, occupy a structurally separate dwelling.

[1] Fitting the equation: Increase in number of houses $= a \times$ Increase in number of families yields a value of 0·98 for a. In other words an increase of 100 families led, on the average from 1801 to 1901, to an increase of 98 houses.

family had any effect upon the amount of building: once again the facts are in harmony with our theory.

Probably the best example of the connection between the variables is seen in the decade 1851–61, during which there was a large increase in the number of families (780,000), a large increase in the number of families per house (1·13 to 1·20), a large fall in the size of the family (4·83 to 4·47), and quite a large increase (490,000) in the number of houses built. One can imagine, on the basis of the theoretical analysis, that the increased number of families of smaller size led to an increase in the number of families per house rather than to a reduction in the percentage of unoccupied houses. In spite of this, there was an increase in the number of houses built, probably because an increase in the number of families would lead to high rents (a contributing factor in increasing the number of families per house) which would lead in turn to increased building.

We must remember, however, that demographic factors are only a few out of many which operate on the demand for house-room, and movements in them can easily be swamped in the short run by movements in economic and social factors. Moreover, each demographic factor helps to determine its partners, and it is impossible to decide which is the cause and which is the effect of building.

3. Building Activity and "Building Need," 1801–1911

What has been the development of "building need" during the last century, and how did actual residential building fluctuate in response? These questions can be answered by utilising the statistics of houses and families given in the Census of Population and already used in section 2.

In 1801 there were 1,633,000 "habitations" and 1,897,000 "families" so that our measure of building need with an ideal standard of one family per habitation was 264,000 "habitations" in 1801. Building need can be calculated in exactly the same way for all subsequent Census years.

In this way, we obtain the results given in Table V, and Chart 2. In Chart 2, the actual building (minus demolitions) is that in the decade following that for which building need is calculated, *i.e.* for 1841 the actual building figure measures the actual building in the decade 1841–51, while building need is measured for the single year 1841. An important point to be borne in mind is that while building

TABLE V

Building Need and Actual Residential Building, 1801–1901

(England and Wales.)

Year.	Habitations.[1]	Separate Occupiers.[2]	Building Need (Col. (2) minus Col. (1)).	New Building Less Demolition.[3]	Deviations of Building Need from Trend.[4]	Deviations of Actual Building from Trend.[5]
	(1) (000)	(2) (000)	(3) (000)	(4) (000)	(5) (000)	(6) (000)
1801	1,633	1,897	264	—	+ 61	—
1811	1,849	2,142	293	216	+ 62	− 25
1821	2,158	2,493	335	309	+ 76	+ 9
1831	2,601	2,912	311	443	+ 24	+ 84
1841	3,117	3,312 [6]	195	516	−120	+ 97
1851	3,432	3,712	280	315	− 63	−163
1861	3,924	4,492	568	492	+197	− 45
1871	4,520	5,049	529	596	+130	− 1
1881	5,218	5,633	415	698	− 12	+ 42
1891	5,824	6,131	307	606	−148	−109
1901	6,710	7,036	326	886	−157	+111
1911	7,550	8,005	455	840	− 56	+ 6
1911 [7]	7,691	7,943	252	No comparable figures available.		
1921	7,979	8,739	760			
1931	9,400	10,233	833			

1 After 1911 " structurally separate dwellings ".
2 After 1911 " private families ".
3 Found by subtracting successive figures in Column 1.
4 Deviations from $y = 28{\cdot}0t + 356{\cdot}5$, where $t = 0$ in 1851.
5 Deviations from $y = 59{\cdot}3t + 507{\cdot}7$, where $t = 0$ in 1851.
6 Simple Interpolation.
7 New definitions of Families and Dwellings were introduced at this date.

need applies to a single point of time, the actual building applies to a 10-year period.

The curve for actual building (minus demolitions) is always above that for the building need in the upper half of Chart 2; this means that if the building need had not been affected by new families and demolitions the actual building during the decade would have been more than sufficient to account for the building need at the beginning of the decade.

But at the same time building need shows an upward trend; actual building was never great enough to keep pace with the increase in the number of families (on the average only 98 houses being provided for every 100 new families). The slope of the new building trend is much higher than that of the building need trend and this indicates that, if new building and population movements continued in the same way as over the century 1801–1901, eventually new building would overhaul building need, the building need would begin to decrease (this would have been somewhere around 1861), and finally would become zero somewhere around 1981.[1]

The straight lines in the upper half of Chart 2 are the trends of building need and actual building, but, for our purpose, the deviations from the trend are relevant; in the long run we should expect that as the building need increases over the century 1801–1901 the actual building will also increase, but it is a matter for verification that the same relationship holds for a shorter period. To eliminate the trends straight lines were fitted to the figures by the method of least squares, the equations being,

(1) Building need, $y = 28t + 357$ where $t = 0$ in 1851.

(2) Actual building minus demolitions, $y = 59t + 508$ where $t = 0$ in 1851.

The deviations from the trends are shown on the lower half of Chart 2; the results prove very interesting. Both curves show the well known long cycles associated with residential building (length about 40 years), and agree remarkably closely from 1801 to 1881. It is not possible to extend the chart up to 1931 since the Census definitions of "families" and "dwellings" changed seriously in 1921. This agreement shows, as might be expected, that "building need" is a dominant factor in the determination of the

[1] The equations of the trends of the relevant series are:

Building need . . .	$y = 28t + 357$
New building	$y = 59t + 508$
Increase in families . . .	$y = 51t + 513$

where t is measured in decades and $t = 0$ in 1851. These equations are sufficient to yield the results given in the text.

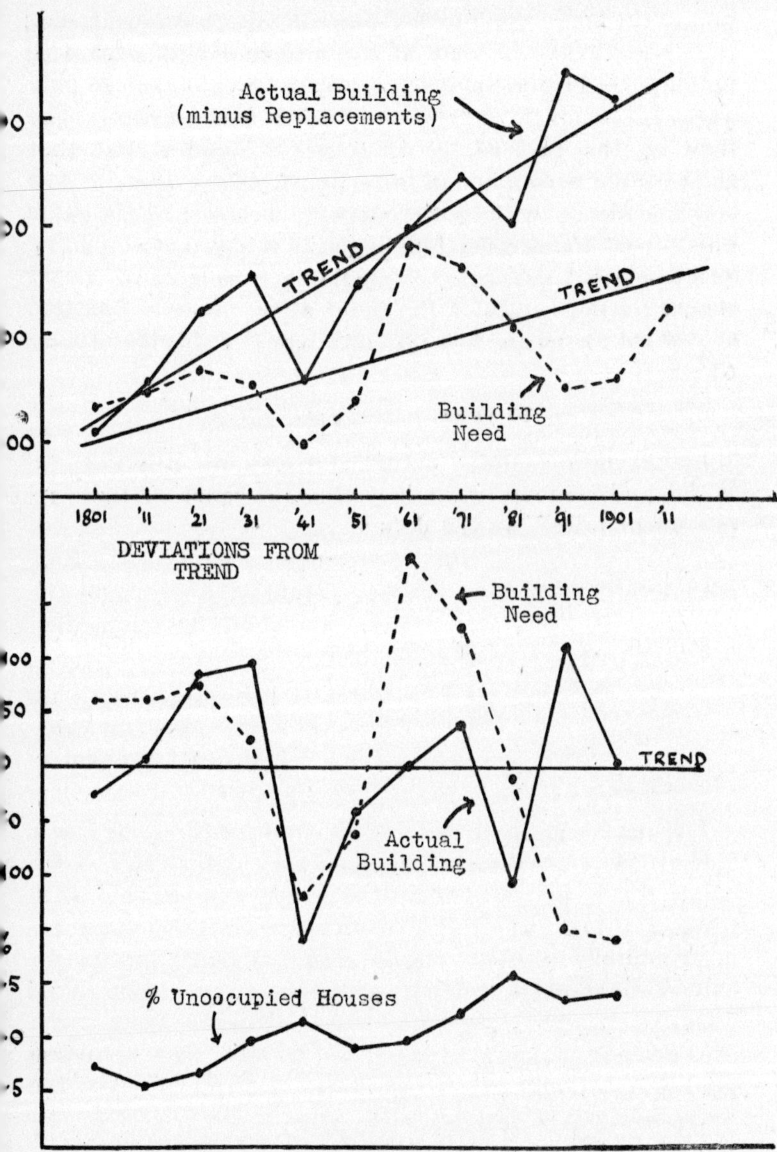

CHART 2

Building Need and Actual Building, 1801–1911.

number of houses built in the long run, *e.g.* 10 years. Indeed it is remarkable, in view of the fact that our measure of building need ignores shifting of population and that we have neglected economic factors, that such a close correspondence between the two curves is actually found. The curve showing the percentage of unoccupied houses shows a close correspondence with both curves: a low percentage of unoccupied houses when building need is high and vice versa. The abnormal rise in actual building from 1891 to 1901,[1] shown by the height of the point above 1891, is probably accounted for by the low rate of interest in this decade (see Chart 4).

4. Future "Building Need"[2]

Let us now examine actual statistics for England and Wales and estimate what has been the value of the "replacement rate"[3] in the decade 1921–31.

	1921.	1931.	
Structurally separate dwellings census . .	7,979,000	9,400,000	Net addition to the number of structurally separate dwellings = 1,421,000.
Structurally separate dwellings actually built 1921–31 . . =		1,616,000	

Annual replacement rate of structurally separate dwellings . $= r = \dfrac{(1{,}616{,}000 - 1{,}421{,}000)}{10 \times 7{,}979{,}000} = 0{\cdot}00244$

[1] Also noticed on pp. 5–8.

[2] Throughout the analysis of future "building need" those assumptions are chosen which yield the greatest number of families in the future. Since all our conclusions based on these estimates arise out of the future *decline* in the number of families, it follows that they are re-inforced by the fact that the decline will almost certainly be greater than that forecasted. For an excellent analysis of the causes of the present change in the number of families (1911–1941) and of the probable building requirements in the decade 1931–41 see the *Housing Report of the Census of Population*, pp. xiii–xx, and pp. lvi–lxii.

[3] The definition of the "replacement rate" will be found on p. 46.

This result may seem remarkable since the replacement rate appears to be so small. But this is probably due to the fact that (i) many houses have been sub-divided into flats during this period, (ii) as the proportion of new buildings in the house population increases, the replacement rate must fall (and many houses were built in the period 1918–21), and (iii) since a derelict old building *reduces* the value of a site, it is often more profitable to erect a new house on a clear site on the outskirts of a city rather than to demolish a derelict house and rebuild, the result being a small proportion of actual replacements. Moreover, the shifting of population will result in fewer demolitions and the " replacement rate ", if measured in this particular way, will be lower on this account.

We now turn to an estimate of the future population of England and Wales made by Dr. Enid Charles.[1] Her conclusion is that the future population will continuously decline. She says : [2]

> " The gross reproduction rate . . . indicates the number of girls that would be born on the average to a woman passing through the child-bearing period, provided fertility remained constant. The gross reproduction rate of England and Wales is now less than unity. The estimated figure for 1933 was 0·845. This means that, whatever changes in mortality ensue, nothing can arrest a continuous decline in the total population, unless something happens to increase fertility above its present level."

Two estimates were made of the future population, one assuming the present fertility and mortality rates to continue unchanged, and the other assuming the present rate of fall of fertility and mortality rates to continue. The first estimate is clearly larger than the latter. For our purpose let us take the upper figure, which is the less alarming, and examine the results of Dr. Charles' estimate.

[1] *London and Cambridge Economic Service*. Special Memorandum No. 40. " The effect of present trends in fertility and mortality upon the future population of England and Wales and upon its age composition," by Enid Charles.

[2] *Op. cit.*, p. 2.

She concludes that the population at different census dates in the future will be as in Table VI. This is her most conservative estimate of the immediate prospect of a fall in the population.

It is important to stress the basic assumption that the fertility rate will not rise in the future. Should it rise the

TABLE VI

Estimation of Future Number of Families

(England and Wales.)

Year.	Total Population.[1]	Percentage over 20 years.	Number of Families.		Increase in Families.	
			(*a*).	(*b*).	(*a*).	(*b*).
	(000)		(000)	(000)	(000)	(000)
1921	—	—	8,739	8,739	—	—
1931	—	—	10,233	10,233	+1,494	+1,494
1940[2]	40,828	70·63	11,310	11,530	+1,077	+1,297
1950	40,678	74·25	12,280	12,360	+ 970	+ 830
1960	39,468	75·45	12,640	11,980	+ 360	− 380
1970	37,343	76·67	12,550	11,450	− 90	− 530
1980	34,614	77·45	12,240	10,730	− 310	− 720
1990	31,559	77·54	11,650	9,790	− 590	− 940
2000	28,522	77·53	11,050	8,843	− 600	− 947

[1] According to Dr. Charles' upper estimate.

[2] In the Census Volume on Housing, 1931, the estimated number of families in 1941 is given as 11,150,000, which lies below estimates (*a*) and (*b*):

(*a*) Assuming that the ratio of adults over 20 per family sinks at the present rate until it reaches the value of 2·0, in the year 2000;

(*b*) Assuming the ratio falls to 2·5 in 1940 and remains there.

whole estimate will be nullified. It is also assumed that there are no wars and that no emigration or immigration is taking place; we must remember that England and Wales are now receiving more and more immigrants each year. On the other hand, changes in the mortality rate would make little difference. However, we can reasonably adopt this estimate in order to determine whether there are likely to be any serious repercussions on the building industry due to the decline in population alone. Before drawing any hasty conclusions we shall have to remember that changes in tastes, incomes and design are likely, in the short period, to swamp the influences of population developments on the amount of building. But if actual building behaves as it did in the century 1801–1901 it will, in the long run, follow the trend and fluctuations of "building need".

If we examine the comparable figures of 1911, 1921 and 1931, for (*a*) the total number of males and females over 20 years of age, and (*b*) the total number of "private families," the following interesting results are obtained:

	1911.	1921.	1931.
Private Families . . .	7,943,000	8,739,197	10,233,000
Males and Females over 20 .	21,683,604	23,883,000	26,997,678
Adults per Family . . .	2·73	2·73	2·64

The decrease from 1921–31 in the number of adults per family is probably due to the fact that in this period so many single-person families were formed owing to migration of young adults and the popularity of flats and thus brought down the average. Now we already have Dr. Charles' estimates of the number of adults over 20 over the next century, so that if we can make an estimate of the future course of the number of adults per family, we can estimate the future number of families. To use this basis seems safer for our purpose than to use persons per family, for we can thus avoid making assumptions about birth rates during the next few years. Two simple assumptions would be (*a*) that the ratio falls at the same rate until it reaches some given limit; (*b*) that the ratio falls further during 1931–40 until it reaches a level at which it stabilises.

We have worked out the results in two ways, (*a*) and (*b*). In case (*a*) we assume the ratio falls until it reaches 2·0 and remains constant at this level. In case (*b*) we assume that the ratio falls to 2·5 in 1940 and remains there. The former case assumes that, ultimately, there are sufficient single-person families to counterbalance all additional adults in families with over two adults per family—a most unlikely state of affairs. The second case seems much more probable. In any case since the information above seems to indicate a fairly stable ratio the number of families is likely to be too high if either of these methods is adopted, so that our estimates will be conservative with respect to the falling off in the number of families. The actual values of the ratio (and therefore the estimated numbers of families) depend, of course, upon the proportion of adult males and females who marry, and the proportion of the unmarried adults who form separate families; it is difficult to say how these proportions will vary in the future. Our results are given in Table VI, but are only considered reliable for one or two decades since it is possible that fertility will rise in the future.

Table VII

Future Building Need

Assuming one dwelling per family as a standard.

In 1921 the number of "Private families" was 8,739,000 and the number of "structurally separate dwellings" was 7,979,000. Hence the building need was 760,000 structurally separate dwellings. The value of r is 0·00244 and is applied to the number of structurally separate dwellings in 1921 (7,979,000).

Year.	Replacement Quota in Previous Decade.	Increase in Families in Previous Decade.	Dwellings Built in Previous Decade.[1]	Building Need.
	(000)	(000)	(000)	(000)
1921	—	—	—	760
1931	195	1,494	1,616	833
1940	195	1,297	1,616	709
1950	195	830	1,616	118
1960	195	−380	—	−67

[1] Assuming the same rate of building as from 1921 to 1931 until there is a decline in the number of families sufficient to offset the building need.

What do these results signify? Seeing that the amount of building activity required over and above replacement and repairs depends, in the long run, upon the actual increase in the number of families, it is obvious that, after 1931, in both estimates (*a*) and (*b*) the increase in families will fall off considerably and even become negative: there should therefore be a considerable slackening off in the number of houses required on this account. On the other hand, if we assume that the replacement rate is the same as in the decade 1921–31, but that it is applied only to those accommodations existing in 1921 and not to those built after 1921, and if we assume the same rate of building as occurred in the decade 1921–31 (it has been even higher in the years 1931–38), we obtain the results shown in Table VII.

At the end of the decade 1950 to 1960 we have the startling result that there will be no need for additional houses—families in that decade will die out in sufficient numbers to wipe out the building need of 118,000 and, in addition, will cause a surplus of 67,000 dwellings. Earlier, we found [1] that the forces at work over the century 1801–1901 would eventually have made " building need " zero somewhere around 1981. Early twentieth-century forces, 1901–1931, speeded up this process until the zero point appeared to be at 1960, or thereabouts. This is a remarkable result, but is admittedly based upon assumptions which are obviously highly hypothetical, particularly in view of the demolition policies of Local Authorities and in view of the fact that we have neglected internal and external migration. But we can test our figures for a part of the first decade 1931–41 by examining the building need and actual building from 1921 to 1939.

5. Building Need, 1921–39

There are no statistics at present showing the annual increase in families in England and Wales. But there are figures showing the number of marriages per annum published by the Registrar-General in his annual reports. The annual increase in the number of families is the difference between the number of new families per annum (*i.e.* the number of marriages plus the number of new single-person families) and the number of families dissolved through death and other causes per annum. Death is likely to be the main factor and it seems reasonable to suppose that the ratio of families dissolved in a year to the number of families at the beginning of the year, a kind of replacement rate, will be fairly stable. Let us examine figures for the four decades 1871 to 1911. The figures for the resulting " replacement

[1] See p. 110.

ratio" for families (an analogy with the replacement rate for dwellings except that it is for a decade) are given in Table VIII. This ratio is obviously fairly stable from one decade to another, though, over the whole period there is a continuous decline. No figures are shown for the decade 1911 to 1921 because of the Great War. The large drop in the

Table VIII

The Replacement Ratio of Families

Source : The Census of Population.

End of Decade.	Marriages in the Decade.	Increase in Families in the Decade.	Replacements During the Decade.	Number of Families at Beginning of Decade.	Replacement Ratio.
1881 . .	1,960,543	584,076	1,376,467	5,049,016	0·2726
1891 . .	2,047,428	497,809	1,549,619	5,633,192	0·2752
1901 . .	2,394,105	905,887	1,488,218	6,131,001	0·2428
1911 . .	2,640,515	918,422	1,672,093	7,036,868	0·2375
1921 . .	—	—	—	—	—
1931 . .	3,024,772	1,493,803	1,530,969	8,739,197	0·1752

Note.—Since the definition of a family after 1921 includes bachelors occupying a structurally separate dwelling the number of marriages alone underestimates the number of additional "families" formed between 1921 and 1931; the "replacement ratio" as calculated above is therefore a lower limit.

decade 1921 to 1931 is due to the large number of new single-person families formed in this decade. The trend of this ratio is probably due to changes in the death rate and length of life. Now, if we assume that the ratio for the decade 1921 to 1931 will apply to the decade 1931 to 1941 and assume that an equal number of families are dissolved annually, we can estimate the annual increase in families from the annual figures for marriages. From these figures and from the figures given by the Ministry of Health for the numbers of structurally separate dwellings built and demolished annually, and on the assumption of the same replacement rate for dwellings, we can estimate the building need for each year from 1921 to 1939. The results are given in Table IX and Chart 3.

In the chart the upper curve of building need is, it must be remembered, merely a historical record of the value

TABLE IX

Building Need, 1921–39

(England and Wales.)

End of Year.	Number of Marriages.	Replacement Quota of Families.	Increase in Families.[1]	Replacement of Dwellings.	Demolitions.	Dwellings Built.	"Building Need."[2]
(1)	(2)	(3)	(4)	(5)	(6)	(7)	(8)
	(000)	(000)	(000)	(000)	(000)	(000)	(000)
1921	321	153	168	19·5	—	39	760·0
1922	300	153	147	19·5	—	111	815·5
1923	292	153	139	19·5	—	92	882·0
1924	296	153	143	19·5	—	86	958·5
1925	296	153	143	19·5	—	137	984·0
1926	280	153	127	19·5	—	173	957·5
1927	308	153	155	19·5	—	218	914·0
1928	303	153	150	19·5	—	239	844·5
1929	313	153	160	19·5	—	170	854·0
1930	315	153	162	19·5	—	202	833·5
1931	312	179	132	19·5	6·5	184	807·5
1932	307	179	128	19·5	6·5	201	760·5
1933	317	179	138	19·5	6·5	200	724·5
1934	342	179	163	19·5	18·2	267	658·2
1935	350	179	171	19·5	30·9	329	550·6
1936	355	179	176	19·5	45·1	325	466·2
1937	359	179	180	19·5	58·4	346	378·1
1938	(359)[3]	179	(180)	19·5	(58·4)	338	298·0
1939	(359)	179	(180)	19·5	(58·4)	(338)	217·9

[1] Found by subtracting column (3) from column (2).
[2] This was equal to 760,000 at the end of 1921. Found by adding columns (4), (5) and (6) to the "building need" at the end of the previous year and subtracting column (7).
[3] Figures in parentheses are assumed values based on the latest value obtainable.

of building need at the beginning of each year, *i.e.* at single points of time. The lower curve, "actual building," shows the amount of building during each year (*i.e.* for 1921, it is the building from March 31st, 1920 to March 31st, 1921) and the area under this curve shows the total amount of

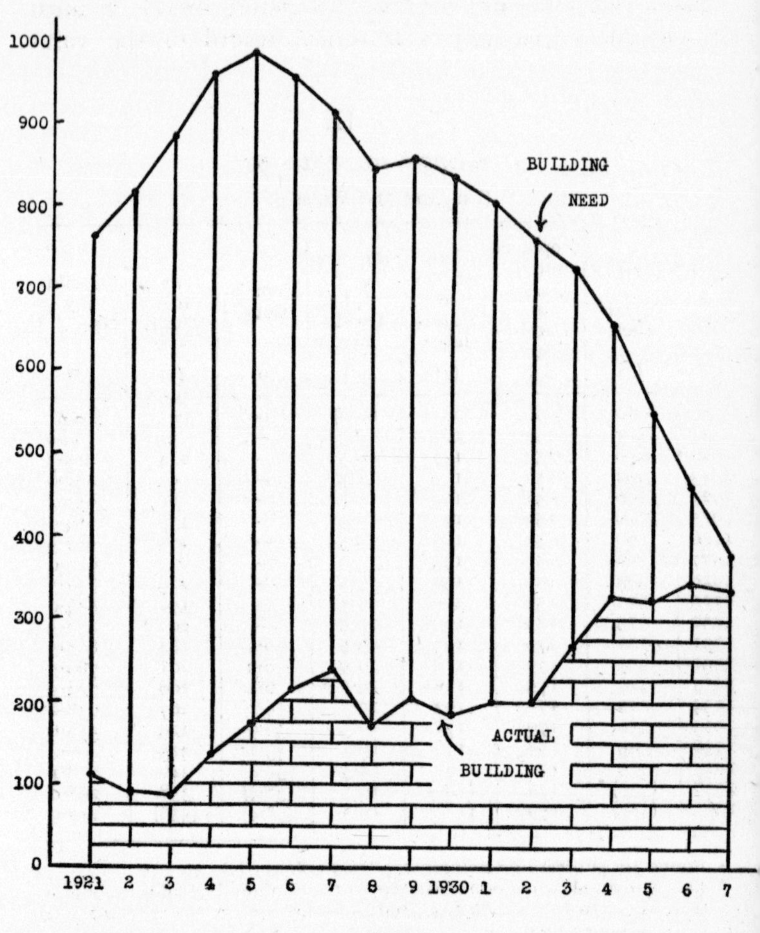

CHART 3

Building Need and Actual Building, 1920–1937.

building over the whole period. The two curves are, therefore, not comparable. But the length of the vertical lines shows the difference between building need at the end of a year and the actual building during the year. If the two curves ever met it would mean that the only building need would be for new families and replacements. The result shown in the chart is striking; there has been an astonishing diminution in the length of the vertical line since 1921 and if the rate of building, which has increased over the whole period, remains at the 1938 level, while marriages, demolitions and replacements do not change markedly, it seems certain that building need will be almost zero at the end of 1941 (see Table IX). An important qualification to these conclusions arises from the fact that our figures for building need are for the whole country and take no account of spatial differences in building need, of spatial movements of population, or of changes of fashion. Furthermore, a single figure certainly underestimates the true building need: simply because it implies that every accommodation is suitable for any family. To be perfectly accurate, separate estimates of building need are required for one-roomed accommodations, two-roomed accommodations, and so on, owing to the fact that each accommodation will accommodate families only up to a certain size. Thus a single figure may hide the fact that there is a surplus of small accommodations and a serious need for large accommodations. But the general tendency and conclusions cannot be seriously affected by these considerations.

Having examined the relationship between changes in demographic factors and changes in residential building over the last century we can conclude that our theoretical conclusions concerning the effects of demographic factors have been amply justified. Demographic factors have been the long run determinants of residential building activity. We have also speculated on the implications for the building industry of the forecasted fall in the population of this country. We find that, unless there are very great internal migrations, very great demolition schemes or serious errors in estimates of future population, there will soon be a marked drop in residential building activity, a drop, moreover, which will not be merely temporary, but which will necessitate a permanently lower scale of residential building and serious reductions in the size of the building industry.

CHAPTER VIII

STATISTICAL ANALYSIS (*contd.*): ECONOMIC FACTORS

HAVING analysed demographic factors, the long-term influences on residential building activity, we now turn to short-term influences, namely, the economic factors. In this case we are able to analyse the causes of variations in factory and commercial building activity also.

1. GRAPHICAL ANALYSIS, 1870–1913

The fluctuations of employment in the building industry (Graph 1), which are some indication of building activity, are shown on Chart 4 to occur more or less in harmony with general business activity as represented by the fluctuations in total employment, wholesale prices and companies registered (Graphs 3, 4 and 5).

Variations in Graph 1 depend upon fluctuations both in residential and in factory and commercial building. The correspondence between residential building and fluctuations in employment in building can be seen by comparing Graphs 1 and 2. On the whole the lowest and highest levels of employment in building occur *after* the lowest and highest levels of residential building. And this seems to indicate that factory and commercial building falls off after residential building and reaches its lowest point when residential building has commenced to revive. In fact residential building seems to revive immediately with and sometimes before business activity in general.

The shaded area in the second graph shows the increase in the number of houses of £20 annual value and over and in Chart 5 the two series (over £20 and under £20) are shown separately. In spite of the fact that as prices, rents and incomes change, this arbitrary division means different things at different times, it would seem that the building of the more expensive houses is a higher percentage of total residential building during the peaks of the major fluctua-

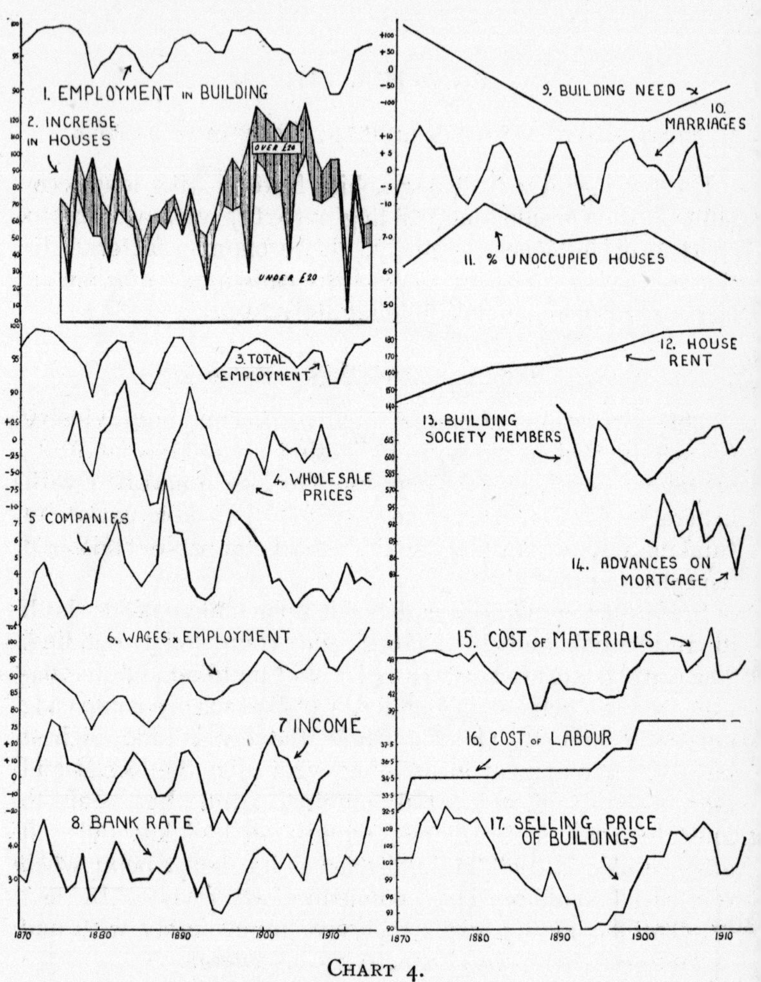

CHART 4.

The Data 1870–1913.

tions (1875–85 and 1895–1909) as indicated by fluctuations in total employment.

The 7-year moving averages shown on Chart 5 show plainly that there have been long cycles in both classes

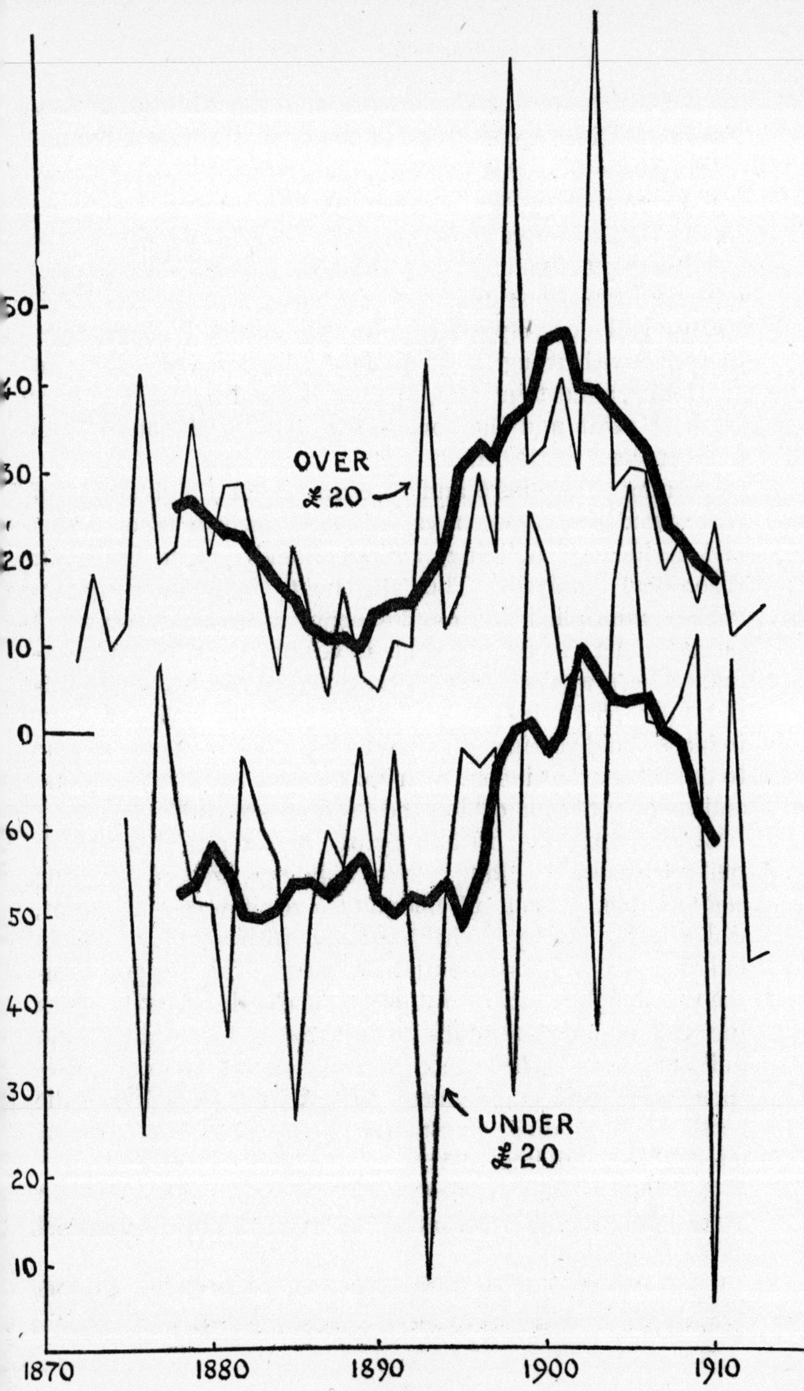

CHART 5.

Annual Increase in Houses of under and over £20 Annual Value (in 000).

though, in the case of houses under £20, there seems to have been no distinct cycle before 1895. The length of these long cycles is about 20 years and, judging from the period before us, the more expensive houses (over £20) begin to increase about 5 years before the cheaper houses (under £20) and also fall a little in advance. Superimposed upon the long cycles are the fluctuations due to the trade cycle. A remarkable feature is the correspondence of peaks of building of houses over £20 with troughs of building of houses under £20, but this is due, almost entirely, to reassessments of annual values in these years and the consequent transfer of houses from one category to the other.

Turning to Graphs 6 and 7 we can detect a high degree of correspondence between variations in income (and wages) and residential building, as we should expect from our theoretical analysis. The agreement between Graph 6 (wages multiplied by employment) and the increase in houses under £20 annual value in Graph 2 is also very striking. The graph showing deviations of marriages from the trend (Graph 10) indicates a high correlation with variations in income and also in residential building. This lends support to the theory that increases in income lead to more marriages and to an extension of demand for house-room.[1]

Graphs 8, 12, 15, 16 and 17 of interest rate, house-rent, building costs and selling price of buildings, are an interesting combination. They all fluctuate (except wages and rent, which are "sticky") in harmony with employment in building and with residential building. This supports our theory that the amount of building is closely linked up with the rate of interest, rents (hence prices of buildings), and building costs. The rate of interest shows the best correspondence with employment in building generally, while residential building fluctuates closely with the rate of interest and building costs.

It is interesting to notice how rent has moved upwards in a straight line, apart from slight waves which agree well

[1] The relationship between real income and marriages has been commented on by Marshall (8th edition, *Principles*, p. 189), Farr (*17th Annual Report of Registrar-General*, 1854) and many others.

with the long cycles of residential construction; when rents are high, construction is high. Cost of labour also shows great "stickiness" but moves upwards in sudden jumps, remaining at the same level for long periods of time.

Costs of building are composed of costs of materials, costs of labour and entrepreneur's profit. It is clear from the graphs that costs of labour are not so variable as costs of materials and it is clear [1] that entrepreneur's profits are even more variable than costs of materials. This is corroborated by the fact that the selling price of buildings (Graph 17) shows greater fluctuations than the costs of labour and materials combined.

"Building need" and the percentage of unoccupied houses (Graphs 9 and 11) show the long period connection of residential building with these two variables.

Building Society membership, and the amount advanced annually on mortgage (Graphs 13 and 14) illustrate the part played by building societies in the period of intense residential building from 1893 to 1910.

These graphs strongly support the conclusions reached, *a priori*, that building activity depends upon those factors set out in the theoretical part of this study. But we have found no indication as yet of the relative importance of these factors beyond our conclusion, in Chapter VII, that the population influences and the proportion of unoccupied houses are long-period factors while the rest are short-period factors.

2. Graphical Analysis, 1924–37

Turning to Chart 6, which covers the period 1924–36, we can see first a decline in building activity (as measured by percentage employment in Graph 1) from 1924 to 1932 and then an increase until 1936. The employment percentage for public works (Graph 2) does not show an increase until 1936. In both industries, however, there was a large

[1] See the leading article in *The Times*, July 6th, 1937, where it is pointed out that out of a rise in price of a non-parlour, three-bedroomed house by £27 in one year, £8 is accounted for by greater costs of materials and £3 by higher wages, the remainder being due to entrepreneur's profit and allowances for rising costs of materials and labour.

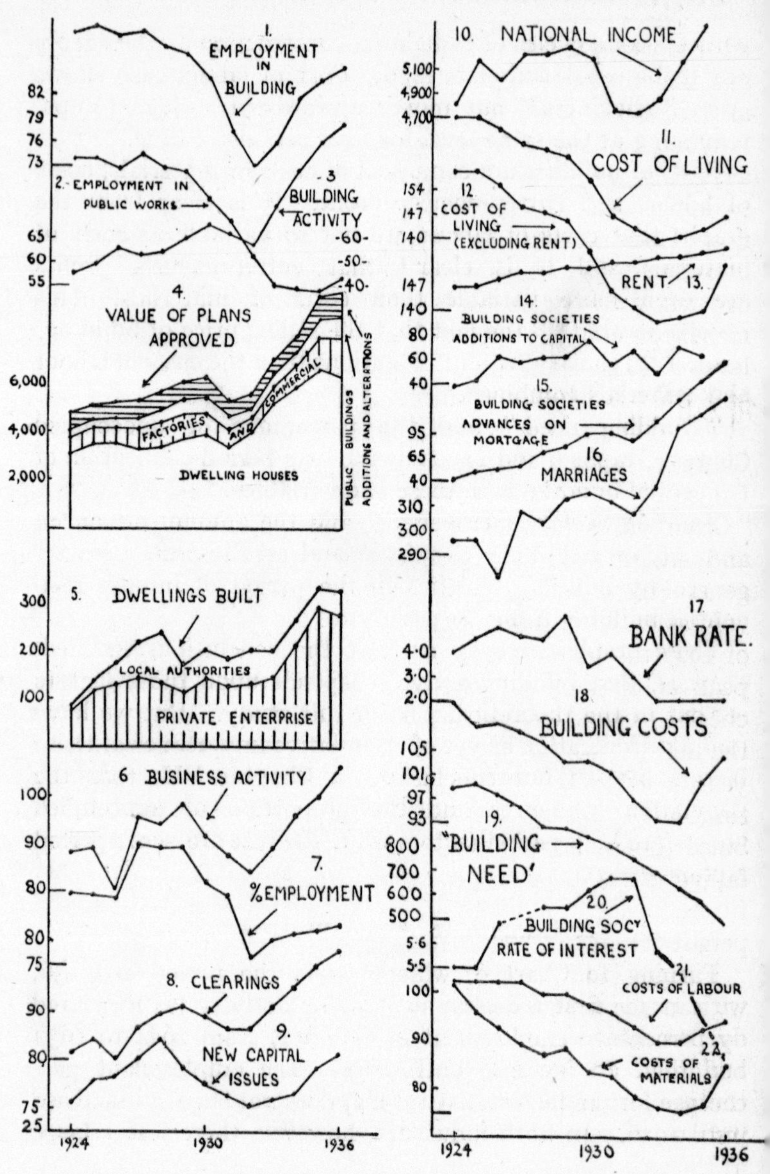

CHART 6.

The Data 1924–1936.

addition to the number of persons insured in the industry, and the employment percentage gives an inadequate picture of the level of activity.

When building activity is estimated in physical terms, by adjusting the value of plans approved with an index of building costs, the picture (see Graph 3) presents an interrupted increase over the whole period, interruptions occurring in 1927, and 1931 and 1932. This makes an interesting contrast with Graph 1, which shows that the level of employment (percentage of insured persons) has not yet reached the level of 1924. This fact is accounted for by the increase of 51% in the number of insured persons between 1923 and 1937. The composition of the plans approved, as shown in Chart 7, is interesting. All four categories, "Dwelling-Houses", "Factories and Commercial Buildings", "Churches, Schools and Public Buildings", and "Additions and Alterations to Existing Property" show the same general movement.

Residential building shows a continued rise from the end of 1927 to the middle of 1930. It was carried beyond the peak of business activity and, indeed, suffered no serious check during the depression years of 1931 and 1932. From the middle of 1932 it mounted steadily until 1935. In that year a setback was experienced, but there was no continued fall and in the middle of 1936 a recovery occurred. Since that date, however, there has been a slow but sure falling off and, bearing in mind our previous estimates of future residential building, it seems that this is likely to persist for some considerable time.

Factory and commercial building shows more harmony with business activity in general and recovered from the depression at the end of 1931 at the same time as residential building. It has, however, maintained its increase beyond the peak of residential building, particularly in the case of "shops, offices, warehouses, etc.", but also suffered a setback at the end of 1937.

Additions and alterations show a movement similar to that of residential and factory building while churches, schools and public buildings display a little more individuality

during 1930 and 1931 by actually increasing until the first quarter of 1931.

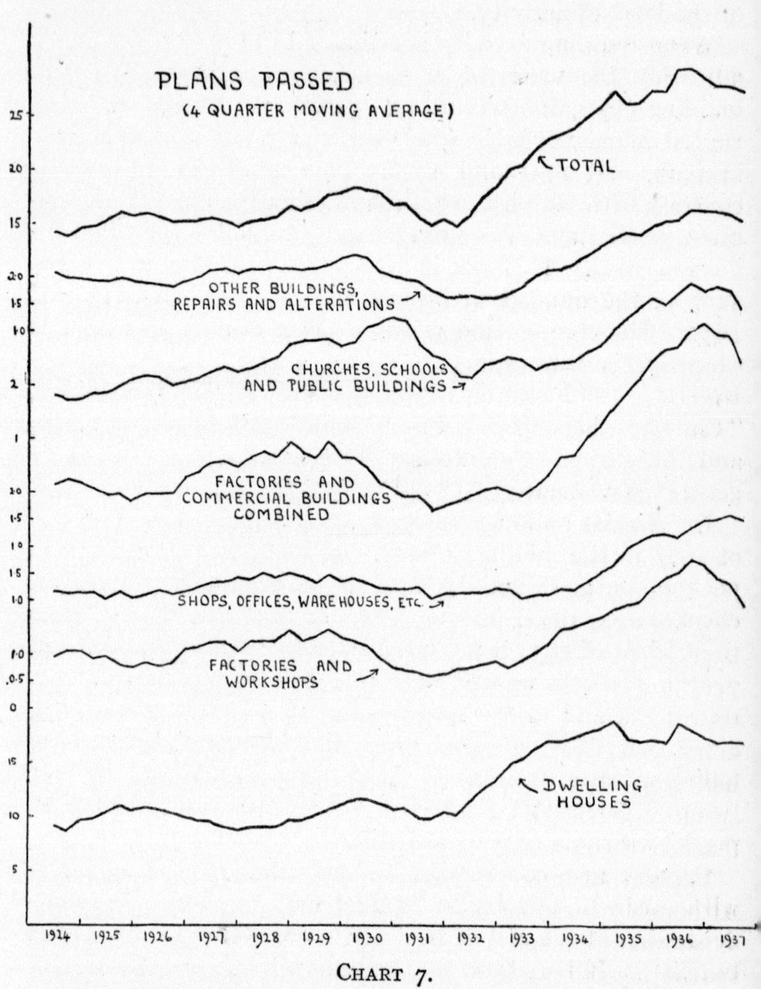

CHART 7.

Composition of Plans Passed by Local Authorities.

Turning to Graph 4 of Chart 6 it will be seen that the proportions in the various categories vary. The "Factories and Commercial Buildings" section shows a broadening out as physical output increases both from 1927 to 1929 and from 1932 to 1937. The same holds true of public buildings and of additions and alterations to existing property. Comparing Graph 4 with the curve for business activity, Graph 6, it is at once obvious that, at the peak of business activity, the proportion of commercial building increases relatively to residential building. This is confirmed when we look at Graph 5 showing the number of dwellings actually built by private enterprise, which shows declines in 1928, 1929, 1931 and 1935–36, while factory and commercial building continued to increase.

Considering the factors connected with residential building, national income (Graph 10) shows a rise from 1924 to 1929 (the drop in 1926 being due to the influence of the coal stoppage), a fall from 1930 to 1932, and a rise from 1933 onwards. The cost of living, and the cost of living apart from rent (Graphs 11 and 12), show a continuous fall from 1924 to 1933 and a rise from 1934 onwards. Rent, however, shows an uninterrupted rise (see Graph 13). On the other hand, building costs (Graph 18) keep falling until 1934 and thereafter begin to rise, while interest rates, as illustrated by the annual average bank rate, and shown in Graph 17 (see also pp. 136–138) show, on the whole, a decline from 1926 to 1933 and remain at a low level for the rest of the period. In view of the close correspondence of these series, on the whole, with movements in residential building activity by private enterprise, there is every reason for believing that they have been important factors in the situation, thus giving additional support to the conclusions reached theoretically.

Population influences also seem to have been important. Although " building need " has shown a continuous decline as shown in Graph 19, we must not forget that it neglects spatial considerations [1] and that it is a long-period factor which started out in 1924 at a very high level. On the other hand, in Graph 16, the number of marriages—an important short-period factor—shows a high degree of correlation with residential building.

[1] Internal migration has remained at a very high level for the whole of this period and has had a very great influence on the total volume and regional distribution of building.

The graphs showing "Building Societies' Additions to Capital" and "Advances on Mortgage" (Graphs 14 and 15) show clearly how important the building societies have been in financing new building during this period. The additions to capital show a slight rise over the period with frequent irregularities and illustrate how the funds of building societies have been continually supplemented. This, as was to be expected, led to lower rates of interest and hence stimulated borrowing. Advances on mortgage are closely related to the number of marriages and the amount of residential building. Note how closely this curve and Graph 16, showing number of marriages, agree with the curve entitled "Building Activity". This correlation indicates that an increase in the number of marriages has led to an increase in residential building activity, financed largely by the building societies.

In the case of factory building the chief factors operating have been shown theoretically to be business activity, building costs, and rates of interest, and once again it is evident from the graphs that these factors are bound up with factory and commercial building.

Building costs are an important factor in both branches of building and it is interesting to see how the cost of labour and of materials, two components in building costs, have varied. From the curves given (Graphs 21 and 22) it is obvious that both have moved in the same way. The costs of materials have, however, shown much wider variation than the costs of labour and we must conclude once again that, though both components moved together and in the same direction to bring about variations in building costs, the variation in costs of materials has been greater than variations in costs of labour.[1] Profits seem to have been at least as variable as costs of materials.[2]

[1] The cost of labour fluctuates with the cost of living, since the scale of wage rates is periodically adjusted on the basis of the cost-of-living index number.

[2] See page 127, footnote 1.

3. Statistical Analysis of Residential Building, 1924–37

The figures giving the value of building plans passed by Local Authorities can be regarded as fairly reliable indications of the monetary value of the buildings which will be built in the immediate future. They clearly represent decisions to build. They are, therefore, the resultants of those forces operating on decisions to build which have been set out in the theoretical part of this study. If we divide the value of the plans passed by an index number of building costs we obtain a figure which roughly indicates the physical quantity of building proposed, or in other words the quantity of building activity measured in physical units which will be required if the plans mature. The figures are split up by the Ministry of Labour into plans for various types of building. They may be split up for our purpose into "Dwelling-Houses" and "Factory and Commercial Buildings", the latter being found by adding "Factories and Workshops" and "Shops, Offices, Warehouses and other Business Premises".

In the case of residential building many of the plans passed will have been submitted by Local Authorities, but we have no knowledge of the exact proportion. However, separate figures are available for the number of houses actually built up to March 31st each year by private enterprise and by Local Authorities, and if we assume that the plans passed in the previous calendar year were in the same proportion we can estimate the value of residential building planned by private enterprise. By dividing this quantity by an index number of building costs we obtain an estimate of the physical amount of residential building planned by private enterprise. Our task is to explain the variations in this variable in terms of those economic factors indicated as the determinants of residential building in our theoretical analysis.

The main economic variables involved are the level of rents R, the cost of building c, the rate of interest i, the national income N, the cost of living L, and the level of business activity in general B. From the first three it is possible to construct an index of an "investment factor"

$$\frac{R}{c \cdot i}$$

which reacts in exactly the same way in response to changes in R, c, and i as we should expect residential building activity to react. We should expect from our theoretical analysis that, if R increases while c and i are constant, annual receipts from ownership of buildings rise while the annual cost remains unchanged. The result is that (*a*) the investor finds investment in residential buildings more profitable, (*b*) rent-payers are tempted to become owner-occupiers by buying houses through building societies or by raising mortgages, and (*c*) both investors and owner-occupiers find it more profitable to put their house into a higher rental class by undertaking repairs and alterations. Similarly if c or i falls while the other two variables remain unchanged the annual cost of building falls while annual receipts remain unchanged, and once more residential building is stimulated. In particular, if i falls and the yields on other forms of investment fall in line with it, investment in buildings becomes even more profitable relatively to other forms of investment. Building is stimulated to an even greater extent. Theoretically, therefore, residential building should be correlated with our "investment factor".

The use of this particular function to represent the "investment factor" must be justified by its success in explaining the facts. It is only one out of many functions which would fit our theoretical expectations, but it is selected here because it is the simplest function which combines three variables into one composite factor and at the same time has a simple meaning if it is the only factor involved. It implies that the elasticity of residential building activity with respect to all three variables is unity. In other words if rents rise by 1%, or if costs of building fall by 1%, or if the rate of interest falls by 1% (*e.g.* from 10% to 9·9%), then in all three cases we expect approximately a 1% increase in residential building activity. Moreover, if all three change by $x\%$ appropriately we expect residential building activity to increase by $3x\%$ providing x be small.

The two variables, the national income N and the cost of living L may be used to form an "income factor" which, it may be thought, has been the predominant one in determining residential building activity in the period we are considering (1924–37).

If we take the monetary national income and divide it by the cost of living we obtain some indication of the level of "real" income. The national income is composed of many items, only a few of which are represented in the cost-of-living index number—which applies to expenditure of the working classes—so this procedure is not strictly justifiable. The resulting index will, however, be a fairly reliable guide to variations in national real income. We should expect, from our theoretical analysis, that the level of national real income would be an important factor in determining the amount of residential building. The greater the real national income the greater the residential building activity. But we must also consider the influence of the relative levels of rent and other prices. If R is the level of rents and L_A is the cost of living apart from rent, the amount of building activity would be expected to vary as $\frac{L_A}{R}$ (assuming a constant real income), since as rents increase relatively to other prices the quantity of house-room demanded will fall. Thus the "income factor" in the demand for residential buildings is, when we also take account of the variations in real income,

$$\frac{N}{L} \times \frac{L_A}{R}$$

Once again we assume, by using this simple function, that the elasticity of residential building activity with respect to each variable is unity over small ranges.

Finally, we should expect, again from our theoretical analysis, that even if both the investment and the income factors remained constant, the amount of residential building activity would vary with the level of business activity. However, in order to simplify our correlations we eliminate the influence of business activity by always measuring residential building activity relatively to business activity in general.

We have now reduced our problem to that of relating three variables,

1. The level of physical residential building activity relative to business activity in general .... $\frac{p \, . \, P}{c \, . \, B}$
2. The " investment factor " .... $\frac{R}{c \, . \, i}$
3. The " income factor " .... $\frac{N \, . \, L_A}{L \, . \, R}$

where,

p = proportion of houses built by private enterprise.
P = value of plans passed (residential).
c = unit cost of building.
B = level of business activity.
R = level of rents.
i = rate of interest.
N = national money income.
L = cost of living.
L_A = cost of living apart from rent.

Before proceeding to calculate correlations there is a fundamental problem which requires solution. That is, the difficulty of choosing a single rate of interest to suit all our requirements, when different persons (*e.g.* investor, owner-occupier and builder) will be influenced by different rates (*e.g.* mortgage rate, building society rate, short-period rate and local bank rate). Shall we choose the national bank rate (annual average), three months' rate, yield on fixed interest securities, building society rate of interest to borrowers, the mortgage rate of interest or some index number of them all?

On Chart 8 five different measures of the rate of interest are plotted. The building society rate on new advances is not published but was calculated from annual figures of (*a*) total interest received during the year, (*b*) the balance of mortgages outstanding at the beginning of the year, (*c*) repayments of mortgage principal during the year, (*d*) new advances on mortgage during the year, and (*e*) average rate of interest on outstanding mortgages. The figures obtained

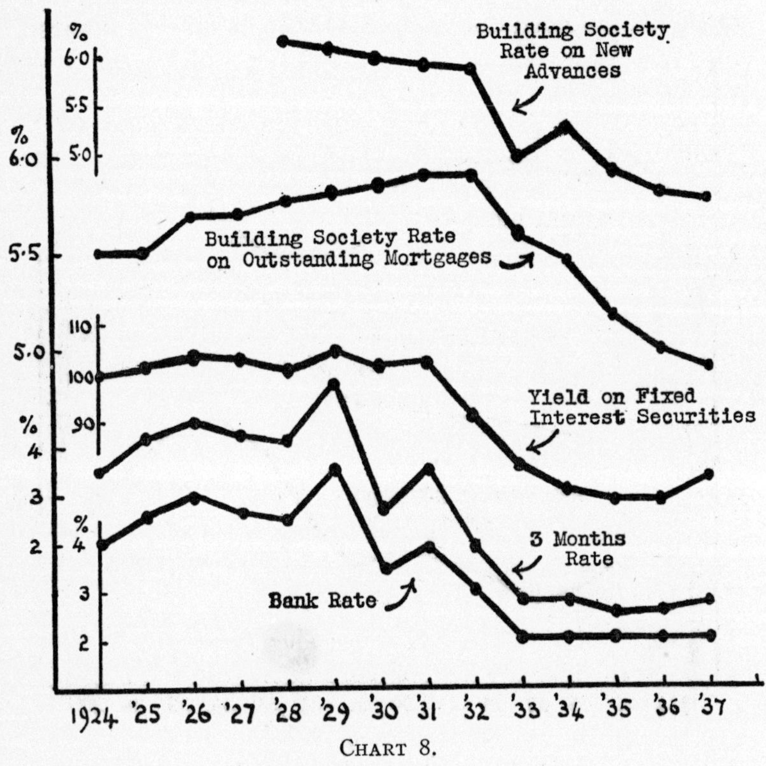

CHART 8.

Rates of Interest 1924–1937.

were only rough estimates of the rate of interest on new advances since certain assumptions had to be made in order to obtain a formula.[1] The general movements in the rate are, however, believed to be accurate.

[1] The formula was: interest received during 1928 = average interest rate on outstanding mortgages during 1928 × (mortgages outstanding at the beginning of 1927 − repayments during 1927 − ½ repayments during 1928) + interest rate on new advances in 1927–28 × (advances during 1927 + ½ advances during 1928).

All five curves show similar fluctuations although the building society rates fluctuate less violently than the other three rates and show a substantial lag. If we chose any one of the rates we should not be far wrong since all are correlated and any one will roughly represent the others. We have decided, therefore, to choose a measure of the interest rate on economic considerations. The long-term rate of interest

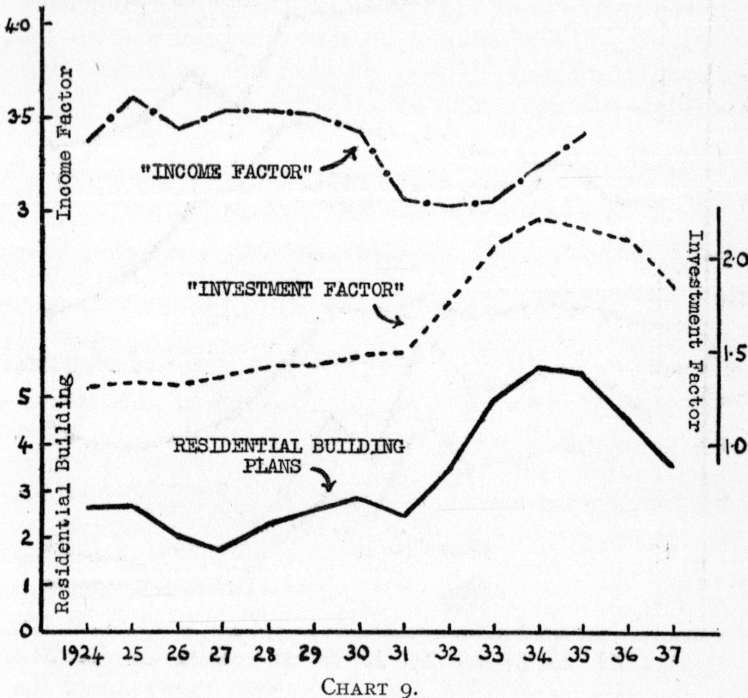

CHART 9.

Residential Building Planned by Private Enterprise, the " Investment Factor " and the " Income Factor," 1924–1937.

(indicated by the yield on fixed interest securities) is certainly the main one in determining the annual cost of a building and, since the interest on capital during erection (borrowed at short term by the builder) is only a small part of total initial cost, the long-term rate was chosen for the statistical analysis which follows. The variations in the three variables, residential building activity, the " investment factor " and " the income factor ", are shown on Chart 9.

In order to investigate every possible relationship between our variables and to ensure that we interpret our correlations correctly we make use of Professor Frisch's " Confluence Analysis ".[1] Those readers who are not at home with correlation coefficients and regression equations are advised to disregard the actual confluence analysis and to resume the argument at the point where the conclusions of the analysis are summarised (pp. 141 and 149). The basis of confluence analysis is the correlation matrix which sets out all the possible correlations between the variables considered. For our data the matrix is as follows (1924–35).[2]

Variable.		Correlation Coefficients.		
		1.	2.	3.
x_1 = Residential building .	1.	1·000	0·969	−0·425
x_2 = " Investment factor "	2.	—	1·000	−0·518
x_3 = " Income factor " .	3.	—	—	1·000

From this matrix it is possible to derive all the possible regression equations between the three variables when taken two at a time, three at a time and so on. Professor Frisch has developed a very ingenious method of displaying all these regressions graphically which he calls " bunch analysis ".

It consists, for any combination of variables, of drawing on one diagram all the regression slopes between the two variables selected for consideration. The tightness of the slopes (or " beams " as they are called) is then an indication of the agreement of the regression slopes as we apply the method of least squares in different directions. By tracing the effects on the " bunches " of beams, of introducing one variable after another into the system (*e.g.* starting with variables 1 and 2 we consider 12, 123, 1234 and so on), it is possible to discover all the valid connections between the variables and to reject all those connections which depend upon "multi-collinearity" (*i.e.* the connection of one variable

[1] Ragnar Frisch, *Statistical Confluence Analysis by means of Complete Regression Systems*. Oslo, 1934.

[2] No figures are available for national income after 1935.

with another merely through the latter's connection with a third). Variables are classified into (*a*) useful variables, which increase the tightness of the bunch and/or alter the

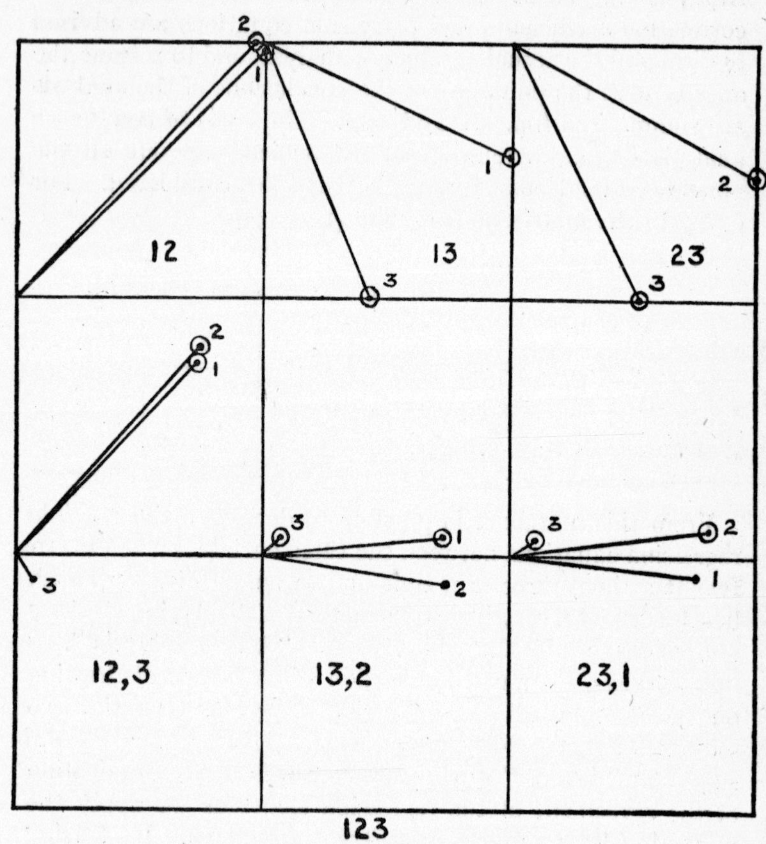

CHART 10.

1. Residential Building Activity (Private Enterprise).
2. Investment Factor (*see* text).
3. Income Factor (*see* text).

slope of the bunch; (*b*) superfluous variables, which leave the bunch unaltered; and (*c*) detrimental variables, which decrease the tightness of the bunch. Many criteria are adopted for the classification of variables in this way but the reader must be referred to the book by Professor Frisch for the elaboration of these methods.

In the case of residential building, Chart 10 shows the results of such bunch analysis. The best correlation is seen in bunch 12 and fairly good correlations in bunches 13 and 23. When 3 is added to the bunch 12 the bunch does not tighten and the direction is unaltered. Further tests all point to the conclusion that 3 is decidedly superfluous.[1]

The conclusion is that x_3 is only connected with x_1 through its correlation with x_2. Since x_1 is clearly connected with x_2, x_3 is correlated with x_1. We must conclude then, that residential building activity depends upon the "investment factor" alone. The "income factor" is not an additional influence but owes its apparent correlation with building to its correlation with the "investment factor".

It is very improbable that real income should have no influence on the amount of residential building. And upon close inspection it becomes obvious that the influence (and the "multi-collinearity") comes through the presence of the level of rents in the numerator of the "investment factor". The level of real income influences the demand for buildings for occupation and ownership and hence the level of rents; the real national income increased steadily by 40% from 1924 to 1935 and the level of rent also increased steadily by about 7%.[2] By including both the level of rent R and the "income factor" we have counted the same force twice—the "income factor" is already fully taken into account in the "investment factor".

In view of these results variables x_1 and x_2 were correlated over the period 1924 to 1937 and a correlation of +0·961 was obtained. The regression equation is

$$x_1 = 3{\cdot}59\ x_2 - 2{\cdot}60.$$

[1] (*a*) The beam 3 falls outside the sector 12, (*b*) the beam 3 is much shorter than beams 1 and 2, (*c*) beams 1 and 2 are not seriously shortened by the addition of 3, and (*d*) beams 1 and 2 in the other bunches in the set are near the zero line and in both cases the beam 3 falls outside the sector 12.

[2] One possible explanation of the low correlation is that the rise in real income during this period has expended its force on the demand for motor-cars, wireless sets, cinemas and holidays—all factors which are omitted from the cost-of-living index number.

The results of this correlation are shown in Chart II. Statistics are also given in Table X for persons wishing to apply the results to future years. It is clear that the "investment factor" explains residential building activity extremely well and that the fit of the equation is very close.

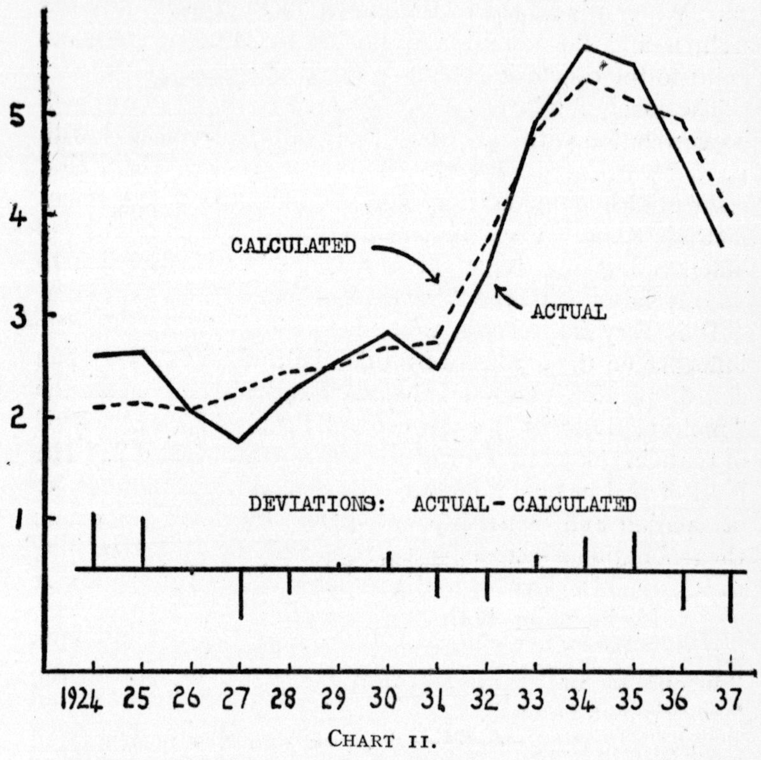

CHART II.

Residential Building Planned by Private Enterprise 1924–1937.

The χ^2 test shows that the probability of obtaining such a close fit by chance is far less than 1 in 10,000.[1] It might be thought that the presence of the variable c in the denominators of both x_1 and x_2 has produced some spurious correla-

[1] Since this was written J. Tinbergen in Chapter IV of his book *Statistical Testing of Business Cycle Theories. I. A Method and its Application to Investment Activity*, has used almost the same variables in a rather different way for Germany, the United Kingdom, the United States and Sweden and for all of them obtains substantially the same results as ours.

tion. Actually, of course, the presence of c in both denominators does not affect the correlation at all but merely serves to make the equation intelligible.

TABLE X.

Actual and Calculated Building Plans.

Year.	Residential (Private Enterprise).			Factory and Commercial.						
	Actual $\frac{p . P}{c . B}$.	Calculated.	Deviations: Actual minus Calculated.	Actual $\frac{P}{c}$.	Calculated. (A).	Calculated. (B).	Calculated. (C).	Deviations: Actual minus Calculated. (A).	Deviations: Actual minus Calculated. (B).	Deviations: Actual minus Calculated. (C).
1924 .	2·61	2·07	+0·54	6·27	7·50	6·99	5·27	−1·23	−0·72	+1·0
1925 .	2·65	2·14	+0·51	5·95	7·79	6·73	6·75	−1·84	−0·78	−0·8
1926 .	2·06	2·10	−0·04	6·01	5·34	6·27	6·31	+0·67	−0·26	−0·3
1927 .	1·77	2·25	−0·48	8·25	9·66	6·48	7·75	−1·41	+1·77	+0·5
1928 .	2·25	2·46	−0·21	9·47	9·23	7·09	9·27	+0·24	+2·38	+0·2
1929 .	2·55	2·50	+0·05	9·82	10·53	6·46	7·56	−0·71	+3·36	+2·6
1930 .	2·83	2·68	+0·15	9·12	8·94	7·25	8·02	+0·18	+1·87	+1·1
1931 .	2·48	2·75	−0·27	6·53	7·36	7·07	7·13	−0·83	−0·54	−0·6
1932 .	3·46	3·72	−0·26	6·73	6·35	9·79	7·23	+0·38	−3·06	−0·5
1933 .	4·93	4·80	+0·13	7·19	7·79	12·08	7·39	−0·60	−4·89	−0·2
1934 .	5·65	5·33	+0·32	9·89	9·81	13·20	10·19	+0·08	−3·31	−0·3
1935 .	5·49	5·10	+0·39	12·98	10·96	13·39	12·98	+2·02	−0·41	0·0
1936 .	4·51	4·90	−0·39	15·10	12·69	13·32	14·60	+2·41	+1·78	+0·5
1937 .	3·52	4·00	−0·48	14·81	14·13	11·90	15·31	+0·68	+2·91	−0·5
χ^2 .	—	—	0·57	—	—	—	—	2·88	8·44	1·49

p = Proportion of houses built by private enterprise.
P = Average monthly value of plans passed (in £00 for residential building and £000 for factory and commercial building).
c = Index number of building costs.
B = Index number of business activity.

There was no evidence of a lag between the two variables. Thus we have grounds for believing that, as far as the data can show, the lag between the "investment factor" and decisions to build is very small.[1] There will, however, be a lag between the "investment factor" and the supply of new buildings for ownership equal to the time required to build (*i.e.* four to twelve months).

4. Statistical Analysis of Factory and Commercial Building Activity, 1924–37

We can approach the problem of explaining variations in factory and commercial building activity in the same way

[1] J. Tinbergen found the same result when he used building permits (U.S.A.) and a 1-year lag when he used the number of houses built (U.K.)

as we approached that of explaining variations in residential building activity. By dividing figures giving the value of plans passed by Local Authorities by the index of building costs we obtain an index of the physical volume of factory and commercial building activity planned. Our

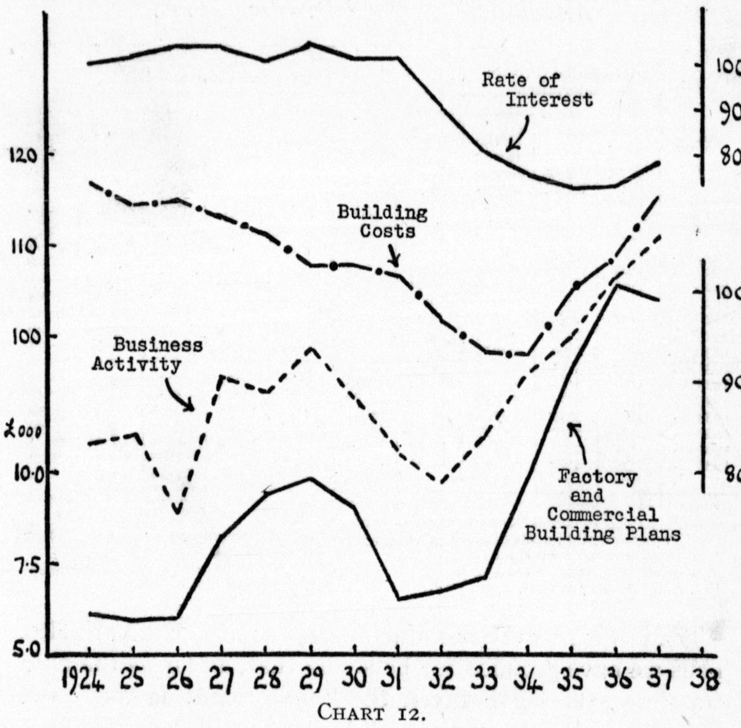

CHART 12.

Factory and Commercial Building Plans, Business Activity, Building Costs and the Rate of Interest, 1924–1937.

theoretical analysis indicated that the main factors influencing factory and commercial building activity are business activity, building costs and the rate of interest. We have therefore considered the following four variables,

1. Factory and commercial building activity .... $\frac{P}{c}$
2. Business activity.............................. B
3. Cost of building.............................. c
4. Rate of interest i

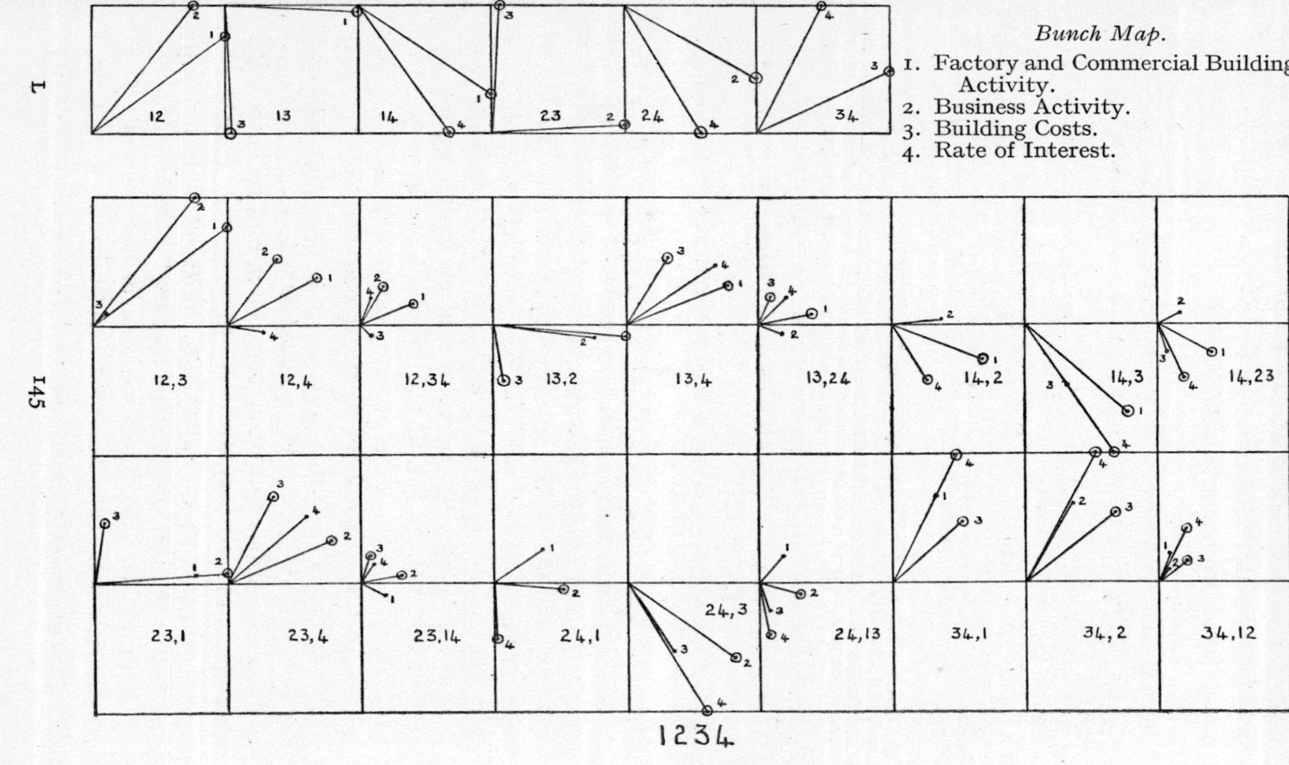

Bunch Map.
1. Factory and Commercial Building Activity.
2. Business Activity.
3. Building Costs.
4. Rate of Interest.
12
13
14
23
24
34
12,3
12,4
12,34
13,2
13,4
13,24
14,2
14,3
14,23
23,1
23,4
23,14
24,1
24,3
24,13
34,1
34,2
34,12
1234

CHART 13.

and once more applied Professor Frisch's confluence analysis. The four variables are shown on Chart 12 and the correlation matrix was (using zero lags),

Variable.		Correlation Coefficients.			
		1.	2.	3.	4.
x_1 = Factory and commercial building .	1.	1·000	+0·762	−0·038	−0·695
x_2 = Business activity .	2.	—	1·000	+0·059	−0·569
x_3 = Building costs . .	3.	—	—	1·000	+0·494
x_4 = Rate of interest .	4.	—	—	—	1·000

In order to facilitate the bunch analysis a " star map " was made from the bunch map of Chart 13. This map is made by examining the behaviour of each bunch as new variates are added and indicating on the map whether the addition is useful, superfluous or detrimental. The star map (Chart 14) is given on p. 147 and shows, for instance, that, if the intercoefficient between 1 and 4 is considered (by examining the column under 14), the addition of variable 3 is useful, the addition of variable 2 is detrimental and the addition of both 2 and 3 as fourth variables (*e.g.* the addition of 2 to the set 14, 3) is detrimental.

The conclusions to be drawn from the star map and bunch map are as follows: (*a*) The best correlation is obtained between x_1 and x_2 (factory and commercial building and business activity). The addition of x_3 (building costs) is superfluous and if introduced would have a very small coefficient, *i.e.* would be of very slight importance. The addition of x_4 (rate of interest) explodes the bunch 12; x_4 is a detrimental variable. This is due to the high correlation between x_2 and x_4, *i.e.* between business activity and the rate of interest. The connection between x_1 and x_4 (correlation coefficient of −0·695) is only through the correlations between x_1 and x_2, and x_2 and x_4. The set 1234 is multicollinear. (*b*) The sets 134 and 234 are " closed sets ". The addition of the remaining variable is detrimental. It is possible that the set 134 owes its fit to the correlations between 12, 23 and 24 and the validity of 134 is therefore doubtful. (*c*) The set 12 has by far the best fit and must be chosen in preference to the set 134.

VARIATE ADDED	INTER-COEFFICIENT					
	12	13	14	23	24	34
1				O		
2		O				
3	O					
1					●	
2			●			
4	●					
1						*
3			*			
4		*				
2						*
3					*	
4				*		
1				●	●	
2		●	●			O
3	O		●		*?	O
4	●	*?		*?		

CHART 14.

Star Map.

* = means that the addition of the new variable has improved the fit of the regression equation; it is a *useful* variable.

O = means that the addition of the new variable has no effect on the fit of the regression equation; it is a *superfluous* variable.

● = means that the addition of the new variable has spoilt the fit of the regression equation; it is a *detrimental* variable.

? = means doubtful.

The fit of the resulting equations,

(A) .... $x_1 = 0{\cdot}288x_2 - 17{\cdot}84$

(B) .... $x_1 = -0{\cdot}042x_3 - 0{\cdot}22x_4 + 33{\cdot}93$

can be seen from Chart 15. It is obvious that (A) is a far better fit than (B) and this is confirmed in Table X where the

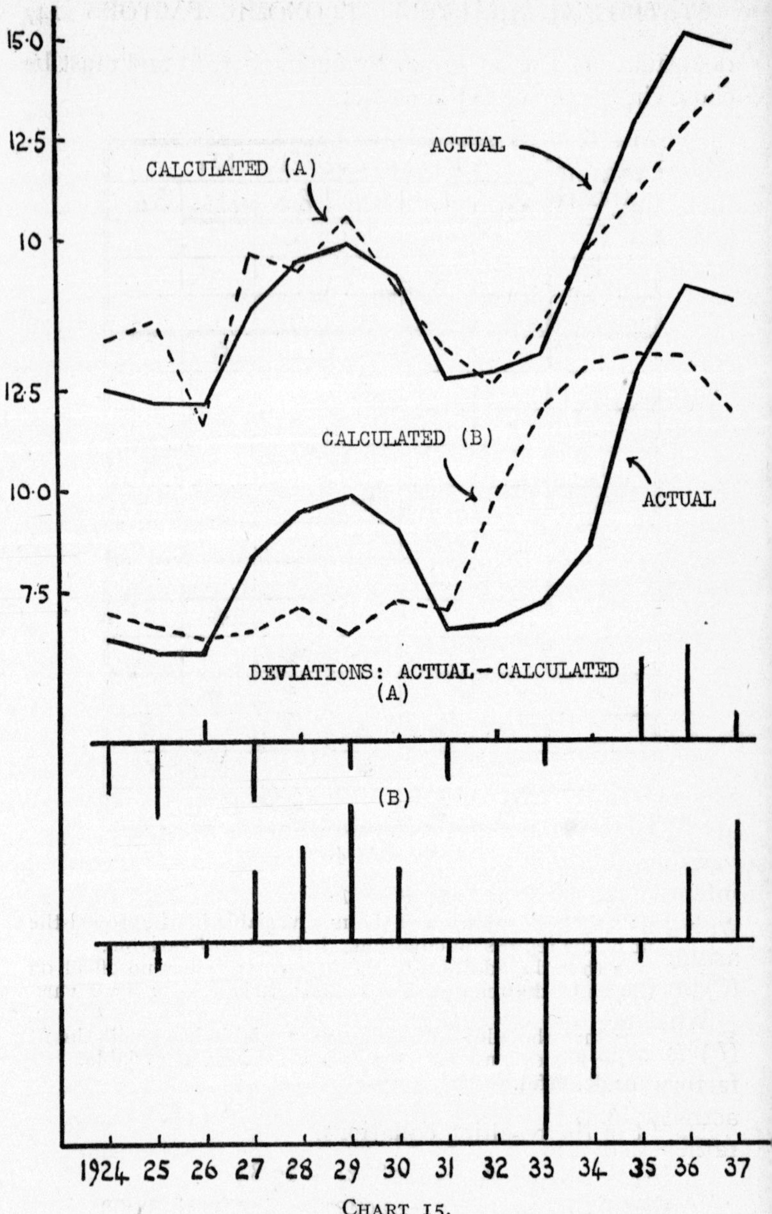

CHART 15.

Factory and Commercial Building Plans 1924–1937.

(A) Correlation using Business Activity.
(B) Correlation using Rate of Interest and Costs of Building.

χ^2 test indicates that, whereas in case (A) the chance of such a close fit arising by chance is less than 1 in 100, in case (B) the chance is not less than 1 in 15. At first sight it might appear that, in case (B), there is a considerable lag between the actual building plans and the calculated building plans and that the low correlation is thus explained, but this is not confirmed if annual changes are inspected. The deviations of the actual from the calculated plans do, however, show a distinct cyclical pattern which seems well correlated with the course of business activity as shown in Chart 12. In Chart 16 it is apparent that, at the downturn of business activity, there is no lag between the deviations of business activity from its trend [1] and the deviations of actual building plans from calculated building plans (B), but that there is a 1-year lag at the upturn of business activity. The correlation is at a maximum of $+0{\cdot}93$ with a 1-year lag and the resulting regression equation is,

(C) .... Deviations (B) $= 0{\cdot}43 \times$ Deviations of business activity from its trend lagged by 1 year.

The extremely close fit of the new equation (C) between actual factory and commercial building plans and the three variables (business activity, cost of building and the rate of interest) can be seen from Chart 16. Table X shows that, with this further refinement, the chance of so close a fit arising by chance is now less than 1 in 10,000. Equation (C) fits the facts even better than equation (A).

What are our conclusions from this analysis? Equation (A) is capable of a very simple explanation. Plans for factory and commercial building depend upon business activity; it is the desire for additional productive capacity rather than the cost of building or the rate of interest

[1] A straight line $B = 92{\cdot}7 + 0{\cdot}84t$ where t is measured in years from an origin mid-way between 1929 and 1930. The value of the index of building activity for 1926 is interpolated in order to avoid an unusually low value on account of the general strike. The value used amounts to assuming that 6 weeks' business activity was lost.

which is important. Furthermore, equation (A) implies that there is no lag between the need for productive capacity and the decision to supply it. The explanation of

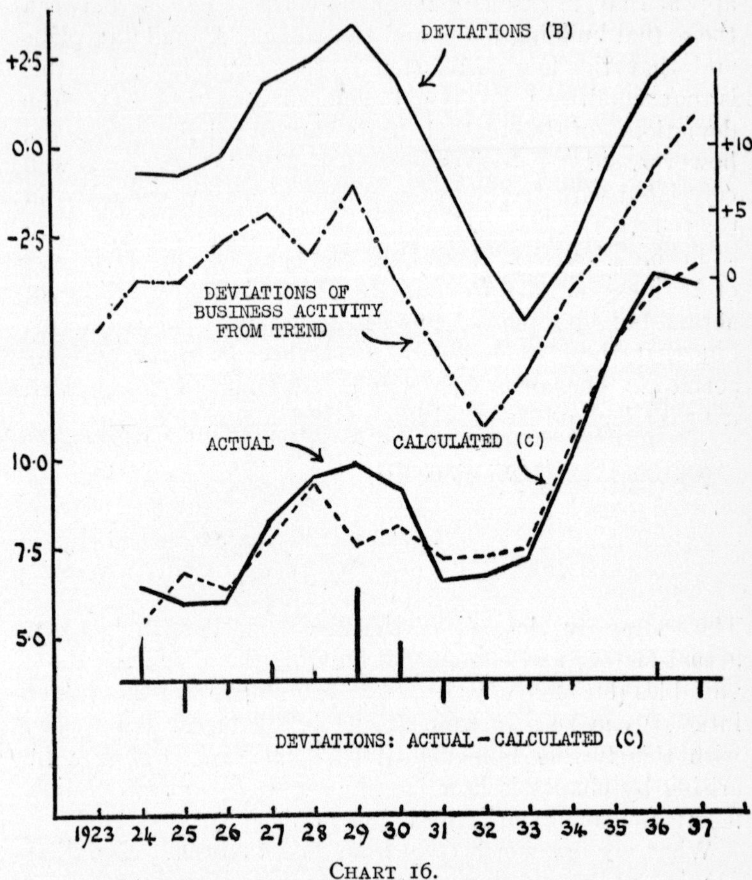

CHART 16.

Factory and Commercial Building Plans 1924–1937.

(C) Correlation using Business Activity, Rate of Interest and Costs of Building.

equation (C) is not so simple. It seems to indicate that, as long as business activity pursues its trend, cost of building and the rate of interest entirely determine (without any lag) the tempo of building plans. But if business activity rises above its trend there is a proposed amount of building in excess of that to be expected from the level of building costs and the rate of interest. And exactly opposite results hold when business activity falls below its trend. Moreover, there is no lag involved at the onset of depression; the fall in business activity leads to an immediate decline in factory building. But it requires a lag of about one year for factory building to respond to the upswing of business activity; probably there is a considerable inertia, in the form of excess capacity, which must be overcome before new factory building responds.[1] Equation (C) does not deny the truth of our interpretation of equation (A) but merely puts a different explanation on the part played by desire for additional productive capacity and recognises the influence of costs of building and the rate of interest. Finally, we must conclude that the evidence of post-war years seems to support equation (C) rather than equation (A).

In deriving equation (C) it is interesting to notice that equation (B) can be written

$$\frac{x_1'}{\sigma_1} = -0{\cdot}083\frac{x_3'}{\sigma_3} - 0{\cdot}894\frac{x_4'}{\sigma_4}$$

where x_1', x_3', and x_4' are deviations of x_1, x_3 and x_4 from their averages and σ_1, σ_3 and σ_4 are their standard deviations. This shows that the relative importance of building costs for factory and commercial building activity is very slight when compared with that of the rate of interest (8% as compared with 89%).[2] The lag between the effective

[1] This diagnosis is put forward very tentatively, since it rests on evidence relating to one depression and one recovery only. We must await several more trade cycles before we can accept it as a general theory.

[2] It will be obvious to the reader that the bulk of this analysis gives results rather dissimilar to the general conclusions of the "Summary of Replies to Questions on Effects of Interest Rates" by J. E. Meade and P. W. S. Andrews in the *Oxford Economic Papers* No. 1. Those replies indicated (*a*) that the long-term rate of interest might have some effect on the demand for dwelling-houses but could have no important effect—that the fall from 6 to 4½ per cent. in the rate on building society advances was not a major influence in the recent building boom, and (*b*) factory building is rarely influenced by building costs or by the rate of interest, but depends upon trade prospects. In any case, building costs and their rate of change are more important than the rate of interest.

demand for additional productive capacity and the *actual* supply of it is, of course, greater than that in equation (C) by the length of time required to build. In recovery it may, therefore, be anywhere between 18 months and 3 years, and in depression anywhere between 6 months and 2 years, according to the size and complexity of the structure.

CHAPTER IX

CONCLUSIONS

We can conclude this study by collecting and summarising the main results which have been obtained from both the theoretical and the statistical analysis.

We have confirmed that changes in the number of families have been the long run determinants of the amount of residential building. Changes in age and sex distribution of the population, with their influence upon the size of the family and its age and sex composition, have been found to be of minor importance up to the present. But throughout it has been constantly impressed upon us that changes in habits and customs and many other subjective factors may be of great importance, and may, in the future, magnify the influence of the above-mentioned factors of age and sex distribution. For in recent years these demographic changes have stimulated and probably will in the future continue to stimulate changes in habits and customs. Thus our premonitions, aired in Chapter VII, concerning the effects of a decline in population and number of families on building activity may need revision in view of these pending changes in age and sex distribution, and in the size of the typical family, particularly in view of the constant technical improvement in accommodations and the adaptation of design to particular types of families (*e.g.* the service-flat for the bachelor). But, in the absence of definite evidence to the contrary, this modification need not be considered very serious. As we have seen, rents are determined by the supply of and demand for house-room, and rents can fall only until they reach a minimum level, which just covers rates and repair expenses. If, at any time, the supply of house-room is increased far beyond the demand for house-room at the existing level of rents, rents will fall to such a low level, and will reduce the amount of new building until, if the process continues, no new building will be carried on. Rents have been "sticky" in the past, but this can only retard such a process and, in the long run, it must work itself out.

There is, however, the possibility of spatial movement of population. If a substantial number moves permanently (*i.e.* long enough to demand additional separate accommodation) from one part of the country to another, then any forecast which considers the number of families alone is obviously inadequate. And such movements would seem to be the most important factor influencing residential building in this country in the future. The people may move in response to changes in location of industry and in response to numerous other stimuli. These factors have been considered in detail in Chapter III and it seems probable that, as economic activity is intensified, controlled by governments, and made the subject of experiment, and as wars and rumours of wars come and go, changes in the future will be more and more speedy and have correspondingly intense effects upon building activity. Movements of the population over short distances are, however, likely to be restrained by the changing of the relative rents of houses in different positions as such movement takes place. Our conclusion for the future is that population trends (decreasing number of families) will tend to reduce the amount of residential building, but this reduction may be offset to a certain extent by other factors such as migration and changes in tastes and incomes and changes in the location of industry. In view of the magnitude of residential building in the last few years, we can safely say that it will soon drop to a very low level and may remain there for some considerable time. Government action and action by Local Authorities with respect to demolition may increase the number of houses which are replaced annually, but this can only postpone, for a time, the inevitable reduction in residential building.

Our statistical analysis seems to show that, in the case of residential building, it is the relative levels of rents, building costs and rates of interest which, almost completely, determine the level of residential building activity relative to business activity as a whole. Thus, residential building is stimulated by increases in rents or business activity, and by decreases in building costs or the rate of interest, but the effectiveness of such changes in any one factor depend upon the levels of the other three at the time of the change. The percentage change in the rate of interest, for example, must be much greater if the ratio

$$\frac{\text{business activity} \times \text{level of rents}}{\text{costs of building}}$$

is small, than if it is high, if the same percentage change in residential building activity is to result.

We have also found that the influence of changes in real national income on residential building activity is fully accounted for by its effect upon the level of rents. There are, at least in modern times, serious competitors with houses for increases in real national income. In the future there may be new competitors, but we cannot speculate here upon future changes due to invention and changes in taste.

In the case of factory and commercial building activity we have offered two related explanations. One explains building plans entirely by the level of business activity or the desire for enlarged productive capacity. The other admits the influence of costs of building and the rate of interest and regards only exceptionally high or low levels of business activity as having any influence on decisions to build, and then sometimes only after a lag. We have found evidence that there is no lag at the downturn and a year's lag at the upturn of business activity. Here again migration of industry is an important factor which cannot be accounted for in any forecast of the future course of factory building activity. By considering business activity as a determinant of factory building we are, of course, avoiding this problem in so far as migration of industry must result in changes in business activity, but the problem is there nevertheless. To forecast factory building activity we must, therefore, forecast future business activity, future costs of building and future rates of interest, and that is obviously impossible in the present state of knowledge.

What is the reaction of the building industry to the trade cycle and does it have any effect on it? It is obvious that most of the variables we have found important for building activity are highly sensitive to cyclical influences. The level of business activity is itself plainly a reflection of the trade cycle. The rate of interest falls during depression and rises during recovery. The cost of building drops in depression and rises during recovery. Rents, depending as they do on real income, tend to fall during depression and to rise during recovery. But since rents are very "sticky" their sensitivity to the trade cycle is not great. As far as residential building is concerned, therefore, it is clear that, unless rents are fluctuating rapidly, our "investment factor" tends to vary inversely with the trade cycle. Residential building activity is, consequently, one of those too often neglected *anti-cyclical* influences which may explain the end and the beginning of depression. It is one of those influences whose cyclical pattern is the reverse of that of the trade cycle. In depression residential building becomes more and more profitable as costs of building and the rate of interest fall until finally it leads out of depression and, through the operation of cumulative processes, induces recovery. Similarly during recovery it becomes less and less profitable until finally it tends to start a downward cumulative process. Factory and commercial building activity may or may not be of the same nature according to which of our two alternative explanations are adopted. If it depends only upon business activity it cannot have much influence on the cycle but is merely a reflection of it. On the other hand if the rate of interest and building costs are as important as was indicated in our alternative equation, it has the same properties as residential building and the same tendency to lead out of and into depression. On the basis of our statistical analysis for the post-war period the building industry seems definitely to possess these anti-cyclical properties. The long cycles of residential building discovered in Chapter VII are an added cyclical influence and when combined with shorter cyclical movements can lead to very violent fluctuations (*e.g.* 1891–1901 and 1932–37). The large size of the industry and its ramifications means that its cyclical influence may easily be transmitted to other industries. It is, therefore, one of the most important industries to be considered in any plan to damp the trade cycle.

One fact stands out from our considerations. We saw in the theoretical section that there is a very large number of demographic and economic factors which determine the level of building activity and that they are interrelated in a complex way. But in practice many of these factors are relatively unimportant. It is apparent from the statistical analysis, at least when considering yearly figures, that a select few of these factors, " building need ", business activity, rents, building costs and the rate of interest, are predominant, and account for the major part of building activity. We have already ventured to prophesy the future—a gloomy future—for residential building, which, after all, depends in the main upon factors susceptible of rational estimation. Factory and commercial building, however, depend much more on unpredictable factors: on spasmodic invention and the incalculable fashions, passions, and fears of kaleidoscopic humanity. In such a field, long-term prophecy can be little better than more or less intelligent guesswork. But for the building industry as a whole, residential building is far more important than the industrial, commercial, and other branches. The future of the industry as a whole is therefore bound up more or less closely with that of residential building. And it follows that, failing some unforeseen stimulus, the industry must be prepared for a period of declining activity.

INDEX OF AUTHORS

SUBJECT INDEX